My worldview greatly evolved as I read this book. Every executive who wonders why his/her company doesn't meet the world's demands should read this book. Keyser's view of "balanced leadership" is truly refreshing; that men and women have complementary skills that significantly improve business. The combination of common sense and real world examples in this book makes it impossible to ignore this fact: innovation and advancement require leadership with both men and women. Obviously, John Keyser understands this.

GLENN A. SPENCER, Chief Operating Officer, Lockton Companies

If we want morale and results to improve in business, senior executives must read this book. We would all be well advised to act upon these messages to strengthen our leadership.

TOM BEGLEY, Begley Law Group

John Keyser has always been ahead of his time. He's been a tireless advocate for women in leadership since he began his career in the 1960s. Keyser has long been a genuine, authentic servant leader - well before those terms entered the business lexicon.

MATTHEW WEY, Managing Director, Marsh & McLennan

A 'must read' for any executive who wants the best possible teams. This book combines hard data with compelling stories from the field to prove that women provide unique and irreplaceable leadership skills that no corporation can afford to ignore.

JOHN M. WALKER, Vice-President & Associate General
Counsel—Litigation, Verizon Communications

John Keyser brings a unique voice and perspective to the national conversation about the advantages of including more women in business leadership. The benefits to business are clear. More to the point, Keyser shows us how to retain and promote talented women into key positions.

GWYN MEEKS, Executive Director, Talent Development, NBCUniversal

John Keyser has written a terrific and timely book. There is wisdom and experience on every page. In addition to topics normally covered by such books, John talks about the issues of working from home and flexible hours. This is a book for men as well as women. John shows us all how men and women can work together for the good of their company. I recommend it highly.

ROBERT LAWTON, S.J., Former President, Loyola Marymount University
and Dean, Georgetown College of Arts & Sciences

A gender-balanced approach to building a leadership team must clearly be a priority in business today. Globally, better-led organizations are continuing to gain market share. I commend John on his work here. Establishing efficient leadership by balancing individual skill sets in the C-suites has clearly been overlooked. John does a great job of articulating, with known facts, how to build successful leadership teams that will in turn create more effective organizations in the decades to come.

KENNETH S. TYRRELL, First Vice President, UBS Financial Services

I highly recommend this book to both men and women in business. Thank you, John, for your insightful support of women in leadership positions. My own 45-year experience in corporate leadership and executive coaching has convinced me that your book is right on target. We need more women in senior leadership--it's the right thing for everyone because women improve culture and performance measures.

AL RITTER, Ritter Consulting Group

This is an extremely well researched and well-written book. Make Way for Women *amplifies the national conversation about increasing women's leadership in the workforce today. By incorporating the viewpoints of both male and female business leaders in his book, Keyser has shown that the companies that embrace gender-neutral hiring, career development and promotion are the most successful.*

JEFF CHAPSKI, Author of *Career-ology: The Art and Science of a Successful Career*

John Keyser's common sense thinking about gender difference in leadership is evident throughout this timely book filled with real stories. Rather than dwell on dismal statistics and why we're not there yet, Keyser and his collaborator, Adrienne Hand, look to a future that is unfolding fast where businesses and the world as a whole benefit from the best and brightest women and men leading together.

ANN GRAHAM, Contributing Editor, Strategy + Business

Make Way for Women *is an excellent source for executives looking to gain competitive advantage by leveraging women's unique skillsets for more balanced, diversified leadership. This book's framework effectively combines empirical research with best practices of respected leaders in numerous fields, from the law to banking to education. Keyser offers a wealth of strategies for taking on the structural and attitudinal barriers women leaders face in their career development and advancement.*

JILL LYNCH CRUZ, PhD, SPHR, GCDF, JLC Consulting, Career Development Coach & Consultant

This book is written for men! So suspend judgment and cross over to appreciate and cultivate the talent of women throughout your organization. Do it for your daughters, your sisters, your wife. Women create communities that offer support and fulfillment for all. Women make teams work!

JOHN FONTANA, President, Fontana Leadership Development, Inc.

Senior executives, both men and women, would be wise to read this book. This is a wonderful collection of insights and advice - from the philosophical to the pragmatic. I was struck by the perfect storm that often exists for women leaders: natural risk aversion, the challenges of primary breadwinner status, and the risk of the glass cliff, as articulated by Cari Sisserson. I especially appreciated Christine LaSala's advice to have confidence in one's strengths, and to realize the importance of trust as a cultural imperative. The clear strategies presented in this book by executives and HR will bring stronger leadership and engagement - and drive financial results.

CAROL MURPHY, Managing Director, Aon Risk Solutions

John Keyser creates a compelling framework and case for integrating women in executive leadership. The men and women profiled in this book are true innovators who value and actively promote the talents and skills of women. Executives who read this book will be able to address the distinct needs of high-potential women and most definitely increase productivity and achieve better long-term results.

RITA CHENG, CEO, Blue Ocean Global Wealth Management

Make Way for Women *is an engagingly written book with a distinct perspective and a timely message. John Keyser exhibits a remarkable understanding of the skills that women bring to the table and to the boardroom, and smartly advocates for the creation of a work environment that allows them to succeed. As a woman in the male-dominated political industry, I can attest to the importance of recognizing, nurturing, and promoting talented young women. This book makes a persuasive argument that when women and men work together in a cooperative, encouraging manner at the highest levels of any industry, the results are overwhelmingly positive.*

STEPHANIE BERGER, President, Berger Hirschberg Strategies

This book is an invitation for leaders of both sexes to join the conversation about ensuring pathways for success at work for all talented individuals regardless of gender—and not because of it, as is the case with men; or in spite of it, as is the case with women.

NICKI GILMOUR, CEO of Evolved People Media, LLC
and theglasshammer.com

This book demonstrates why successful firms work with John Keyser as a leadership coach. His extensive real world experience managing teams and large organizations is as evident in his writing as it is in his counsel. He is a clear thinker with a unique perspective. This book is well organized and entirely comprised of actual cases confronted by women in business today. John's analysis and advice are clear, practical and easily applied. As the father of two young women I am grateful to see someone – a man - acknowledging the challenges they will confront, and recognizing the unique leadership value they have to offer.

BILL CURTIS, Porter & Curtis

This book has important messages about the multitude of strengths and skills that women bring to business leadership, and clearly shows how empowering women to use these skills will create winning cultures in our companies. John Keyser and the men and women interviewed in this book provide important insights and practices for organizations looking to become more effective, decisive, and profitable.

J. ROCK TONKEL, CEO, Arlington Asset Investment Corp.

MAKE WAY FOR WOMEN

MEN & WOMEN LEADING TOGETHER
IMPROVE CULTURE AND PROFITS

JOHN P. KEYSER
WITH ADRIENNE HAND

LIBRASTREAM

BUFFALO, NEW YORK

Hardcover ISBN: 978-1-68061-000-0
Trade Paperback ISBN: 978-1-68061-001-7
Ebook ISBN: 978-1-68061-002-4

BUS109000 BUSINESS & ECONOMICS / Women in Business

Publisher's Cataloging-in-Publication Data

Keyser, John P. (John Patrick), 1937-

Make way for women: men and women leading together improve culture and profits / John P. Keyser with Adrienne Hand. -- Buffalo, New York : Librastream, [2015]

pages ; cm.
ISBN: 978-1-68061-000-0
Includes bibliographical references and index.
Summary: This book builds the case that businesses and organizations need men and women together in senior leadership positions to bring out the best in their people and to maximize consistent results. Numerous business leaders address the issues and challenges facing women in the workplace and present forward thinking solutions that make their organizations stronger with women in key leadership roles. Helping women advance is not only the right and just thing to do, it will also have very significant favorable effects on growth, services and profitability.--Publisher.

1. Women executives. 2. Leadership in women. 3. Businesswomen. 4. Leadership. 5. Executives. 6. Human capital. 7. Industrial management. 8. Success in business. 9. Corporate culture. I. Hand, Adrienne. II. Title.

HD6054.3 .K49 2015   2015936725
658.4/092082--dc23   1504

Librastream
520 Franklin Street
Buffalo, New York, 14202

First Edition
Printed in the United States of America

WRITING THIS BOOK HAS BEEN QUITE A JOURNEY, thankfully a pleasure, because of the inspiration I received from those we interviewed. The men and women profiled in this book are highly respected in their fields and with very good reason. They are servant leaders who care deeply about their coworkers. They are also forward-thinking leaders who truly understand the value of sharing leadership among men and women.

When I originally planned this book, my thought was to interview highly renowned executives, because I believed their fame would help influence and deliver this message to the men in the corner offices today: sharing leadership with accomplished women will strengthen your company and your culture and improve financial results.

I was naive and quickly realized that I would gain more information and insight from the experience of leaders in diverse fields who would sit with Adrienne Hand, my editor, and me for an hour to discuss their experiences. Sure enough, these conversations were fascinating and fully conveyed the value that women are bringing to organizations, leadership, and people.

As I wrote this book, I had the great benefit of having Adrienne Hand as my editor. She is an accomplished writer, has no personal agenda and is easy to work with. She put up with me!

I hope this book is a success as the messages from the leaders included in the book are critically important and need to be shared with today's senior executives. I hope they will process these messages and become forward-thinking leaders, out front of the change that is coming.

I dedicate this book to my wife, Leland, who suffered through the hundreds of hours spent writing, rewriting, researching and discussing the manuscript. Her patience and support are dearly appreciated.

I also dedicate this book to my son, Kevin, and daughter, Leigh Lalich. I love them dearly and could not be prouder of their character.

And I dedicate this book with love also to my sisters, Carol Mercer and Noel Fischer, and to my stepson, Alex Beckel, and stepdaughter, MacKenzie Beckel.

I hope this book is well received because the messages are so important. Please know that it was written with love and humility.

—*John Keyser*

CONTENTS

FOREWORD

Women are a vital part of business. In my field, finance, women are some of the industry's best leaders. They don't try to distinguish themselves right away. Instead, women are often more concerned with results than recognition.

In my experience, women create successful work environments. When there's a balance between men and women in leadership, it's better for teamwork. When there are enough women, there is a willingness to help each other. It's about raising the tide to raise the boat.

"Connect, Then Lead," a 2013 Harvard Business School study, showed that the best way to gain influence is to combine warmth and strength.[1] Personal connection develops trust and promotes the inclusive exchange of—and openness to—ideas. Women bring these qualities to leadership in our companies. It seems to me to be commonly accepted that women want to understand how employees feel. They create a sense of teamwork while achieving desired results. They encourage their team members rather than using intimidation. Women tend to reach out to colleagues to create a more satisfying work environment. This is critical to reducing turnover.

Many women have had to work hard and make sacrifices. They have to balance responsibilities at work and at home. They recognize the importance of flexibility, and know that flexibility increases employee satisfaction. We can take advantage of today's technology and offer people the flexibility they need. This will heighten organizational spirit and produce outstanding results.

My advice to women is to have confidence. Not overconfidence, but quiet confidence. Be confident enough to admit mistakes and move on. Don't be afraid to fight unpopular fights. Marissa Meyer made a very hard decision. Yahoo's performance has risen significantly under her leadership.

My advice to men is to be leaders in promoting talented women. As much as we like to believe things are equal, they're not. Compensation has gotten better for women, but not enough. According to the U.S. Census Bureau report there is still a 23% difference (U.S. Census 2012).[2] Despite every Fortune 500 company reporting they are pushing for female advancement and equality, most companies are still very male dominated.

This is an important book. A successful female business leader encouraged John to expand an article he wrote about balanced leadership into a book. She told him there are hundreds of books by women for women in business, but to her knowledge, there was not one book written by a man with credibility in the business world, telling male executives that they have an opportunity to be progressive leaders by advancing women to leadership, while also improving their companies' cultures and financial results.

Morale in the workplace is low across the country. Talented women can help men change that by joining senior leadership and helping us to be more engaged, helping our people feel appreciated and valued, and ultimately helping to drive improved financial results. Diversified leadership is required to attract and keep high-potential women who want success in their professional and personal lives. This will also help attract and keep today's very talented young generation, Gen Y, the Millennials.

Johnny Williams, Vice Chair, UBS

PREFACE

Let's face facts: companies with women in senior management have stronger results. Companies with the highest representation of women in top management have 35.1% higher returns on equity and 34% higher total return to shareholders.[3] Gender-diverse leadership groups simply outperform others, by a large margin.[4]

Yet women's key leadership strengths and skills continue to be undervalued and underutilized. I have been a senior executive for more than forty years, working side by side with very talented men and women. Now, in my leadership coaching and consulting business, I work with hundreds of men and women who are striving to improve their skills. A great many of the highly effective people I have worked with throughout my career are women. But time and time again, women are overlooked for promotion to very senior positions.

A great many of the highly effective people I have worked with throughout my career are women. But time and time again, women are overlooked for promotion to very senior positions.

In this tough economy, we are doing our businesses an injustice by having all male or predominantly male leadership. We've got to wake up and realize that women make up half the workforce and 51% of management and professional positions; women influence 80% of buying decisions; and yet women are only 13% of executive committee level positions, and just 5% of CEO leadership.

As David Chavern, of the U.S. Chamber of Commerce says, advancement is not a gender issue, it is an economic issue.

"Advancement in business is not just a 'women's issue,' it is an economic issue," according to David Chavern, president at the U.S. Chamber Center for Advanced Technology and Innovation.

Look at the success women are bringing to Yahoo, IBM, PepsiCo, Hewlett-Packard, Kraft Foods, DuPont, Deloitte, Ernst & Young and others. Sure, women and men tend to have different leadership strengths, and that's just what we need in today's very competitive business world: complementary skills and knowledge. In today's economy, it is imperative to provide the strongest possible leadership by combining the leadership strengths of men and women, so that we can maximize our services and improve financial results.

I wrote this book to encourage men to step forward and include more talented women in key leadership positions. Forward-thinking men and highly capable women can expedite this vital culture change together. This is a real leadership opportunity to join with other progressive business leaders who are working side by side with female executives and bringing in greater returns.

Forward-thinking men and highly capable women can expedite this vital culture change.

So let's get out in front of the change that is coming! Be seen as a leader and recognize what is right and best for your company. You will definitely enjoy better culture and stronger financial results by including women in your leadership!

So let's get out in front of the change that is coming! Be seen as a leader and recognize what is right and best for your company.

In this book we profile senior male and female leaders and discuss the key strengths of women's and men's leadership styles and skills. We establish how much more energized and loyal people are when leadership captures our combined strengths. We present the business case for promoting women to leadership, citing statistical and anecdotal evidence that companies jointly run by women and men are profiting. You'll see that an increasing number of male executives realize that promoting women to leadership is a business imperative.

Reading this book, you will hear from suc-

In this book we establish how much more energized and loyal people are when leadership captures our combined strengths.

cessful male leaders who have the wisdom to share leadership with women. These men describe the positive impact that women's leadership has had on their colleagues, their cultures and their results. You'll hear how women are strengthening business in numerous fields.

You will also hear from exceptional female leaders who describe how they bring a positive influence to the culture of their organizations and drive better results. These are women who have succeeded in male-dominated environments by adding value to culture and generating revenue. They have important messages for senior managers and women who aspire to success in business.

As we interviewed these talented businessmen and women for this book, we heard again and again that women are stronger and clearer communicators than men. We heard that women address important issues, ask more questions and are more thorough in discussions. Business leaders told us that women do not race to bold decisions—instead, they consider the potential long-term effects of risks, and they are inclusive in decision making.

This book proposes strategies for successful gender-diverse leadership.

I doubt that we would have suffered so many financial institutions tanking and losing billons of dollars of their investors' money if there had been more women in key leadership positions.

Yes, we need women in the C-suites and in other key positions. They complement men's skills, making for a stronger, risk-aware and collaborative leadership team.

This book proposes strategies for successful gender-diverse leadership. We demonstrate how leadership that engages people brings high performance, loyalty and excellent results over time. We know that when companies put employees and clients and customers first, their employees are satisfied, their clients and customers are loyal, their profits increase, and their continued success is sustained.[6]

We specify how companies can be more family- and mother-friendly with flexible scheduling and, especially, with trust and empowerment, so that women and a growing number of men can stay connected with clients, colleagues and work while raising children.

We support FWA, flexible work arrangements, in which productivity matters more than hours at a desk in the office.

We learn strategies from highly capable human resource, organizational development and talent management professionals Lisa Loehr, Lulu Gonella and Emily Holland White, who tell us how to implement policies that attract and especially retain talent. We hear proven strategies for advancing women into key executive responsibilities and enhancing work-life balance. We talk about measuring contributions by results, not hours worked. That means we must be willing to be flexible and trusting whenever possible, taking advantage of technology to communicate and to work remotely. We hear from young professionals who work in virtual offices and demonstrate the effectiveness of this growing trend.

Just as women have learned from men's leadership, we must learn from theirs.

Writing this book has reinforced my belief in women's leadership. As Sheryl Sandberg said in her book *Lean In: Women, Work and the Will to Lead*, we must all work together to understand what is holding so many women back. We must learn directly from women whose talents and skills already add so much depth and breadth to our companies. Just as women have learned from men's leadership, we must learn from theirs. In my experience, confirmed by the business leaders in this book, women focus on people in addition to the bottom line. They have conversations, they ask purposeful questions, they listen to understand and to learn, and they let people know they are appreciated and valued. By doing so, women create high-performing cultures and drive results.

We cannot exclude the competencies of more than half of our population.

If you read this book with an open mind, you will realize that it's essential to have women in leadership positions. Striving for balanced leadership must be an absolute top priority. We cannot exclude the competencies of more than half of our population. Our companies, our people, deserve the strongest leadership possible. Combining the leadership strengths of women and men will vastly improve our companies and meet the challenges of this demanding economy.

PART I

THE BUSINESS CASE FOR WOMEN IN LEADERSHIP

IN THIS SECTION WE LEARN what women bring to the table. We discuss women's specific leadership strengths, how they complement men's leadership, and how men and women leading together greatly improve morale and productivity—and drive profits.

We also learn why women are not advancing to leadership. What is causing this drain of talent? And how should leadership respond? We look at specific solutions, including a progressive program at Deloitte that clears access through the pipeline.

If we want to lead our companies well into the future, we must all work toward solutions that create equal opportunities for women and men to advance to leadership.

1

WHAT WOMEN BRING TO THE TABLE

In my work as a leadership coach and consultant, I hear a lot about what women are bringing to the table. The COO of a large financial services company recently told me how much he values his female senior executive, not only for her outstanding business skills but also because she is highly attuned to the people in the organization. He regularly seeks her counsel for her wise perspective on internal relations. A CEO of a major consulting firm says his most reliable senior partner is a woman. When she tells him she will finish the project by a certain date, she always delivers.

These business leaders value the skills women bring to the executive level. They are demonstrating what has been proven: When women and men lead together in the C-suite, the levels of intelligent problem solving and innovation rise significantly, according to a 2011 *Harvard Business Review* research study of 7,280 leaders by Jack Zenger and Joseph Folkman.[7]

What are the specific skills women bring to leadership? Risk awareness, strategic long-term thinking, loyalty, flexibility, strong communication skills and patience, among others. Women also tend to excel at collaboration and empathy. What does this mean? It means that women are often better at connecting with customers, teammates and stakeholders. Take a look at John Gerzema's extensive research that links traditionally feminine traits such as empathy and collaboration with effective team engagement, in *The Athena Doctrine: How Women (and the Men Who Think Like Them) Will Rule the*

When women and men lead together in the C-suite, the levels of intelligent problem solving and innovation rise significantly.

Future.[8] This excellent book concludes that companies are best led jointly by women and men, because both skill sets have an important place at the table.

Where men tend to be bold and make quick decisions, women tend to be thoughtful and collaborative.

Throughout my career as an executive and now as a leadership coach, I have consistently found that women balance men's leadership skills. Where men tend to be bold and make quick decisions, women tend to be thoughtful and collaborative. Where men focus on goals, take risks and drive for results, women look at the big picture, gather input and collaborate to build sustainable organizational cultures that achieve long-term results.

In executive committee meetings, men keep the group moving toward the goal, and women consider issues and perspectives that would improve the outcome, assuring the result is sustainable and that the long-term effect on their people is favorable.

There is a powerful synergy of talent that raises productivity and morale. Together, men and women in the C-suites are driving profits. Research by high-tech venture capital firm Illuminate Ventures shows that tech organizations with the most women in top management achieve 35% higher return on equity (ROE) and 34% better total return to shareholders.[9] In the McKinsey study *Women Matter*, companies with 20% or more representation of women on boards had 26% higher return on invested capital.[10]

There is a powerful synergy of talent that raises productivity and morale. Together, men and women in the C-suites are driving profits.

Women are performing at the executive level. Zenger and Folkman write that 67% of women in senior management excel at taking initiative, driving for results, retaining talent, customer satisfaction, employee engagement and profitability.[11]

McKinsey & Company's 2012 leadership study, Unlocking the Full Potential of Women in the U.S. Economy, shows that women excel at intellectual stimulation, setting expectations and rewards, inspiring their people and inclusive decision making.[12]

Consider these facts:

- 60% of U.S. college students and 70% of college valedictorians are women.

- 51% of women are in middle-management positions. Organizations with the most women in top management achieve 35% higher return on equity (ROE) and 34% better total return to shareholders.[13]

Yet:

- The fifty highest-paid executives in the U.S. are all men.

- Men are still paid approximately 25% more than women for the same work.

- 28% are VPs or senior managers.

- 16% are on executive boards.

- 14% are in top management and executive committee positions.

- 5% of Fortune 500 CEOs are women.

Bypassing women for promotion is unfair and unwise. It is harmful to our businesses and our all-important organizational cultures. So why does this practice continue?

There are numerous reasons that there are too few women in leadership positions. Biased hiring and promotion practices are a part, but there are other reasons. For one thing, there are too few role models. Women need to see other talented women in leadership who show them the way. Also, women are often excluded from informal networks formed by men, the old boys' club. And too many women do not have a sponsor in upper management to create opportunities. Or, if they do, they are not being advised to develop financial and business knowledge, or to improve their sales and business growth capabilities—even though this is exactly what men are advised to do. Men are told that in order to advance in their careers, they must demonstrate strategic and financial acumen that brings results. 50% of middle management is missing out on this crucial step to leadership. That 50% is women. Men are shown the business, and women are encouraged to gain confidence and build networks. No wonder more women are not advancing![14]

In my work, I have found that the most limiting factor in women's rise to the top is poor judgment. Managers—male and female—are often not even considering high-potential women for promotion because they assume that a woman can't handle the job and family obligations as well as men. Also, many women hold themselves back, believing that they don't have the right skills yet. Others are just waiting to be asked.

In Deloitte's 2010 study *Unleashing Potential: Women's Initiative Annual Report,* they determined the reasons why so many talented women were leaving the firm. Women were leaving because of a lack of role models, mentors and flexibility, and because of assumptions they would not be able to handle tough assignments. Fortunately, as a result of this study, opportunities at Deloitte were equalized for men and women and the necessary support was put in place for women.[15]

> Managers—male and female—are often not even considering high potential women for promotion because they assume that a woman can't handle the job and family obligations as well as men.

What exactly did Deloitte do to create equal opportunities for women? Here's one of their programs worth replicating at your company. High-performing women and men senior managers were selected to participate in a five-month class designed to deepen their understanding of the business and strengthen their client service and leadership skills. They worked closely with senior leaders, learning how decisions are made and evaluating how better to execute key strategic initiatives. In the end, each of them developed recommendations to present to the CEO. Since 2001, 166 senior managers have used this opportunity, and as of 2012, fifty of the participants are partners, principals or directors.[16]

It is true that some women choose to opt out of opportunities for promotion because they are prioritizing family responsibilities such as child and or elder care. Others may stay in jobs where they feel a deep sense of meaning professionally. Some may value close relationships with their colleagues, and the way they work together to make a difference. They may feel they will lose that feeling of connection and satisfaction if they rise to the next level with endless meetings and the often-present corporate politics.

Let's realize, though, that most women aren't opting out of the workforce—most cannot afford to. And sometimes high-performing women hold themselves back not only because of family responsibilities, but also to add more balance to their lives by volunteering and pursuing other interests.

One of the objectives of this book is to offer ideas as to how companies can accommodate high-performing and high-potential women so that they may pursue success in business as well as satisfaction in their family and personal lives. I know there are plenty of men who also wish for work-life balance. Many executives might react to this idea by thinking that business is so demanding that it takes great sacrifice and long hours to be a senior manager today: "That's just the way it is." To them, I counter that it is not just the way it is, not if we want to improve our results.

> **Leadership has little to do with hours. It's about inspiring people to do their best. It's how we make people feel.**

And yet it seems that the measure of good management is the hours spent in the office, traveling, in meetings, on conference calls and speaking with other senior managers. That is founded on the assumption that extensive hours mean strong management. That is absolutely untrue.

Leadership is helping others do the right things well. It's inspiring and energizing a team to achieve common goals. Leadership has little to do with hours. It's about inspiring people to do their best. It's how we make people feel.

But we must not be doing it right, when 70% of our employees do not feel fully engaged, and a great many who don't feel appreciated are either actively looking or would consider leaving for another job. According to Gallup's *State of the American Workplace* report in 2013, that costs our economy $450 billion in lost productivity.[17]

We have to address this. The status quo is simply not working. We are not doing a good job with leadership that is overwhelmingly male.

Remember, our results over time are determined by the collective commitment of our people. Yes, we can drive them to achieve annual goals for a while, maybe a year or two or even three, but if they are not engaged, enthused and happy, we will lose them either physically or mentally. If they lose their passion for their work, their pride in their company, and their respect for their boss and senior management, either they leave or the quality of their work declines.

As Gretchen Spreitzer and Christine Porath write in *Harvard Business Review,* when people feel part of an energetic, collaborative team, and when they feel their work makes a difference, productivity and retention go up.[18] The most successful teams generate that special sense of vitality, camaraderie and shared purpose that is so motivating and personally satisfying. Creating this sense of satisfaction is something women do very well.

Yet time and time again I hear CEOs and senior executives rationalize turnover, ignoring its real cost, which is many times the annual salary of the person who left. I repeatedly hear that people today do not have the same work ethic, the same passion, and that she or he wasn't really that good anyway. (Really, then why were they with you for six years?)

We keep hearing that our poor economy is caused by jobs going overseas, to China and other countries where wages are so much less. Yes, that is true, and yet I believe if we provide our businesses with strong, gender-balanced leadership, our financial results would greatly improve, and so would our economy. Highly effective leadership is the key to long-term financial success.

People currently in top positions must stop making assumptions and shortsighted thinking.

To help improve leadership that raises morale and productivity, we've got to combine the strengths of both women and men. People currently in top positions must stop making assumptions and shortsighted thinking, such as:

- "We cannot find the right women."

- "If we put a woman in that role and she does not do well, it'll set back all women."

- "A woman isn't right for that role."

We must determine what leadership skills we need to stay competitive, and open our minds to the fact that men and women bring a critical balance to leadership. There is a school of thought that recommends against generalizing. I understand that. Yet, from my experience I am convinced that to understand and appreciate the differences between men and women's skills is to begin the important work of improving business leadership and financial results.

Let's take a look at men's natural leadership skills, and then we'll see how they relate to women's skills. In general, men are:

- decisive

- bold

- confident

- risk aware

- charismatic in business

Are these skills important in leadership? Of course! These skills help drive results and hit financial targets. Businesses want breakthrough results and they want to sustain them. But if we recognize that our long-term results are based on our organizational culture—the attitude, spirit and enthusiasm of our people—how do we feel that these pragmatic skills are helping our people to love their work, to have pride in our companies and a desire for outstanding teamwork?

Men's skills are more about driving for results than about engaging people, yet that is essential for long-term success. That is why leadership needs to be diversified. Women tend to focus on people and relationships more than men do. Now, let's look at women's leadership skills. In general women are:

- appreciative

- excellent communicators

- inquisitive

- good listeners

- inclusive

- long-term thinkers
- risk aware
- ethical
- loyal
- caring

> **Our emotional intelligence skills allow us to develop and maintain solid relationships that are founded on respect and trust.**

These qualities and skills are every bit as important as the qualities and skills we normally expect from men. For example, women are inclined to raise an issue when something is not ethical. In my experience, women will not sit by and let unethical or bad behavior carry on. In favor of expediency, men might be inclined to accept or ignore things that are wrong for the company and for people in the company. I have seen this perspective lead to short-term business decisions or inaction, and long-term harm. Research supports this observation.[19]

TalentSmart, a global think tank and consultancy that is a world-leading provider of emotional intelligence tests and training, found that women excel on three of the four core emotional intelligence leadership skills: self-awareness, social awareness and relationship awareness. Men and women score about the same on the fourth skill set, self-management.[20]

This is very telling. Emotional intelligence is a key indicator of success in business, in leadership and in happiness in our personal lives. Our emotional intelligence skills allow us to develop and maintain solid relationships that are founded on respect and trust. And business is all about relationships. The sounder the quality of our relationships, the more success we'll likely achieve.

Some of you might be saying, "I don't have time for this." In our crazy busy business world today, we spend most of our time in meetings, at our computers and on the phone. In a great many companies, the pressing business of the day requires that the CEO and the chief officers of operations, finance, technology, marketing, human resources and organizational development talk to each other a great deal of the time. We don't think we have time to get out of our offices, off our floors, and talk with the people doing the work at our companies. But that is an important part of our responsibility. We must reorganize our priorities and make the time!

Relationships are built on conversations, asking people how they are doing, asking how we can help, and letting them know we genuinely care!

As you will see when you read this book, women make internal relations a priority. They initiate communication and are thorough in discussions. Women are far more apt to leave their offices, walk the halls and have conversations. This leadership style is very important to the people of a company. People want to be asked for their ideas. Women are most often the ones who ask, listen patiently and let their team members know they are appreciated.

Solid, productive relationships cannot be built using emails, newsletters and conference calls. Relationships are built on conversations, asking people how they are doing, asking how we can help, and letting them know we genuinely care!

Let's remember the best ideas are usually bottom-up ideas. Do you want something improved? Ask the people doing the work how to improve it.

Because of their high emotional intelligence, women are more inclined to initiate

Women help people feel good about themselves, their work and their company.

these conversations, to let people know that their ideas are important and to thank them for their work. This is absolutely the reason that women's leadership has very positive effects on the people of a company. Women help people feel good about themselves, their work and their company. This leads to a winning organizational culture and spirit that drives outstanding client service and sustains breakthrough results.

Please understand that I am not espousing leadership by women only. We do not need exclusively male or female leadership. We need leadership that combines the best qualities, skills and competencies of women and men. It's time to open the doors to the C-suite and build the strongest, most effective leadership teams to drive results, build morale and keep good people. Now is the critical time for men to mentor, coach and sponsor women who can contribute more to their companies. Women have the skills necessary to keep people engaged and highly productive. To stick with the status quo—businesses run predominantly by men—is to ignore the leadership strengths of more than half of our population, workforce and college graduates. If we ignore the impact that women are making in business today, we are limiting progress and failing to maximize our long-term profits.

> **Now is the critical time for men to mentor, coach, and sponsor women who can contribute more to their companies.**

Managers focus on numbers; leaders focus on people and numbers. My message to my male colleagues is if you want to be a great leader and you want your company to thrive, bring talented women onto your leadership teams and give them the freedom to use their instincts and skills along with their business growth capabilities. Provide the same professional development for both men and women in order to capitalize on their combined leadership strengths. Promote women to the C-suite and watch your organizational culture and financial returns improve.

Let's open the doors! Let's be fair and do the right thing. We must all recognize the value that women bring to leadership. We must all work toward 30% women in leadership, at a minimum. According to Linda Tarr-Whelan's research in *Women Lead the Way*, a single or two women in leadership often feel that they must "go along to get along," and their voices are not heard or heeded as much. With at least three women on management committees, their contributions resonate and our results improve.[21]

Let's make it a corporate imperative and give incentives to our managers who promote talented women. Women reflect the diversity of our client base. They bring expertise, efficiency and inclusive leadership to the workplace—adding tremendous value to culture and the bottom line.

Be a forward-thinking leader. Be in front of the change that is coming.

2

WOMEN AND MEN TOGETHER
DRIVE PROFITS

There is now definitive evidence that sharing executive leadership with women is driving profits. Women in the C-suites are exceeding targets at IBM, PepsiCo, Hewlett-Packard, Kraft Foods, DuPont, Yahoo, Deloitte, PwC, Campbell Soup and Ernst & Young, and the list is growing steadily.

McKinsey & Company recently partnered with The Wall Street Journal's Executive Task Force for Women in the Economy to analyze the impact of women on profitability. In their study of 60 companies that have successfully increased the number of women in leadership, more than 80% of the HR leaders said that gender diversity is a business imperative. According to the study, 90% of CEOs said, "We are getting the best brains to work on problems." They also said that it's essential to have a workforce that is competitive in markets where women are making most of the purchasing decisions. When asked for metrics to verify the return on investment, one senior executive told researchers, "It's common sense— those who tell you they need more evidence are just looking for an excuse not to act."[22]

There is now definitive evidence that sharing executive leadership with women is driving profits.

Promoting talented women to executive positions makes business sense. As we've demonstrated in the previous chapter, women create positive, loyal and highly productive cultures. Women's thoughtfulness and thoroughness in executive committees balance men's boldness, leading to decisions that favor long-term profitability.

You've got to reflect your client base to succeed in today's diverse marketplace. In my work, I hear about numerous companies diligently preparing for presentations and failing to win orders when the prospective client has women at the table and the presenting company is all male. Women influence 80% of buying decisions in the marketplace, from new homes to cars to PCs; and women control $20 trillion, or 70% of total consumer spending globally.[23]

It just makes business sense to include women in the leadership of businesses. Since women make up over half of today's workforce and are driving spending and profits, it is clear that companies should do whatever it takes to recruit and retain talented women.

If we look at the big picture, we can see that many companies are not doing well financially, and few companies sustain outstanding financial success. In fact, too few companies endure. It's shocking how few companies are 100 years old. When my former company, Johnson & Higgins, celebrated our 100th anniversary, it was a big deal for us and for Chicago. The mayor came to an event to congratulate us on live TV. From the chamber of commerce, we obtained a list of other companies that were 100 or more years old and were amazed at the scant number.

Since women make up over half of today's workforce and are driving spending and profits, it is clear that companies should do whatever it takes to recruit and retain talented women.

And now Johnson & Higgins is gone, as well as other companies that were household names—Continental Bank, Philco, Plymouth, Spalding, Chemical Bank, Manufacturers Hanover, Lehman Brothers, E.F. Hutton, Shearson Hammill, Bache, Oldsmobile, Gimbels, Ralston Purina, Bear Sterns, Singer, RCA, Magnavox, Sinclair, Swift, Borden, American Motors, Armour, Bendix, Borg Warner, American Cynamid, Tidewater Oil, Esso, Decca Records, Eastern Airlines, Pan Am, TWA, Crown Zellerbach, Bonwit Teller, Garfinkels, Gimbels, Best & Co., Riggs National Bank, Arthur Andersen, Coopers Lybrand, Korvettes, Sylvania, Howard Johnsons, Home Insurance Company, Reliance, Singer and hundreds of other well-known companies. These companies either are no longer in existence, are now part of another company, or are no longer of the significance they were in the past.

There are thousands of lesser-known companies that no longer exist. Many would say this is because of less-than-stellar management. So, how do we turn this around? Start by recognizing that women have sharp business skills that are critically important. Remember that women are more risk aware than men. Business leaders should be bold and take prudent risks. However, it is important to think through potential actions. What's the upside, what's the potential downside, and what are the adverse effects of failure on people down the road?

We know that women balance men's leadership styles, open up decision-making analysis, bring important perspectives and care for the people doing the work of the companies. With an increase in the number of women in leadership positions, the spirit and sustainability of a company improves.

Take a look at someone who is improving culture. Edith Cooper has been the global head of human capital management at Goldman Sachs since 2008. She is responsible for the well-being, development and promotion of Goldman's 32,000 employees worldwide. Like many HR executives, Cooper says, "Our people are our number one asset." Many companies say this, but Cooper and Goldman are acting on that commitment.

"We've emerged from what was one of the most challenging periods of financial services history, and we've come into a better, more normalized position. We've been able to take a step back and really think about the future," says Cooper.

Cooper is responsible for recruiting the best talent for Goldman Sachs, which remains one of Wall Street's most sought-after investment banks. In 2014, Goldman Sachs was named one of Fortune's 100 Best Companies to work for.

"This is a dynamic business, and our priorities evolve alongside the markets," she says. "As a result, there is an increased focus on managing people, leading people and leveraging the diverse set of experiences that our people bring to the table."

Still, there are not enough women at the top. We must remember that having a woman in the room for the sake of having a woman may not improve results. There must be at three or more women in the C-suites and on executive committees. Why? Because having three or more women present in senior-level meetings and on boards opens up thinking, reflection and thoughtful discussion, and that is when better decisions are made. How do we know this? Take a look at a recent Catalyst study.

Catalyst's report, "The Bottom Line: Corporate Performance and Women's Representation on Boards," shows Fortune 500 companies with three or more women board directors had significantly higher financial performance than those with the fewest women board directors.[24]

This study, which is the second of Catalyst's Bottom Line reports, looked at return on equity, return on sales and return on invested capital, and compared the performance of companies with the highest representation of women on their boards to those with the lowest representation.

According to Ilene Lang, former president of Catalyst, "This study again demonstrates the very strong correlation between corporate financial performance and gender diversity. We know that diversity, well managed, produces better results. And smart companies appreciate that diversifying their boards with women can lead to more independence, innovation and good governance, and maximize their company's performance."

Fortune 500 companies with the highest representation of women board directors have significantly higher financial performance than those with the fewest women board directors.

I totally agree that women bring tremendous leadership skills to boards of directors. I feel strongly that it is equally important to have at least 30% women in C-suite and field leadership, because women connect with the people doing the work of the company.

Here's a case study that shows the business advantage of having 30% women in leadership. In 1993, Deloitte realized too many women were leaving the firm and not enough of the women who stayed were advancing to senior levels. So management created a systematic development process called Women's Initiative (WIN). As of 2014, 35% of partners and 30% of directors at Deloitte are women. The company credits its success to the combination of male and female executive talent. "We view attracting, retaining, and developing women as more than the right thing to do—it is a business imperative that fuels our growth.-[25] This success can be replicated at other companies.

> **As of 2014, 35% of partners and 30% of directors at Deloitte are women. The company credits its success to the combination of male and female executive talent.**

Let's commit to improving our leadership in business so our team members are happier and more engaged, and so our financial results will consistently improve.

In this chapter, we will hear from leaders who report on the fiscal advantage of sharing leadership with women. We hear from Steve Steppe, then–managing partner of RReef, who convinced his other partners to bring the first woman onto the board. Steve knew that her talent in the real estate investment business and her ability to manage people would bring tremendous value and profit to the company and their people.

Peter Johnson, former IMG CEO of sports and entertainment, shares how he knew that tennis star Stephanie Tolleson would bring phenomenal value to the company. He understood that in sports marketing, the best approach to serving and recruiting clients is to introduce a strong team from the outset—to employ and empower people of both genders with different skill sets, personalities and backgrounds.

Stephanie Tolleson—whose list of accomplishments is endless, including an $88 million contract, the largest ever for women's sports—expands on this story, aptly pointing out that women in leadership positions tend to place more importance on morale, which is very important!

Finally, we hear from Grant Davies—managing partner of Davies

Consulting, a highly successful consultancy in the energy field—who has worked with many talented women since the 1970s. Grant argues that employees and shareholders all benefit with talented women in leadership because of the positive differences they make.

STEVE STEPPE

Steve Steppe is the executive managing director and co-head of Stockbridge Capital Group, a firm whose portfolio comprises approximately $6.4 billion of assets across the investment risk spectrum and also provides strategic advisory services with respect to real assets and portfolios. Steve's personal and professional experience has made him a strong supporter of women in leadership. Steve feels he had an advantage when he was young because he grew up with a working mother. "I got a head start," he says, "understanding the importance of promoting women in organizations." His experiences with the women he has worked with have also given him enormous respect for the leadership that women bring and the differences that they make in a company.

> **"Clients like to do business with firms that treat women and men equally. They look for firms with both men and women in senior positions."**
> **—Steve Steppe**

"In the investment management field, especially the pension field, a lot of consultants are women," Steve says. "Clients like to do business with firms that treat women and men equally. They look for firms with both men and women in senior positions. It is just a good way to do business, especially in the service industries."

Steve believes women deliver profits and bring stability to discussions at his firm. He says men tend to get aggressive with each other and say things they regret later. But when there are women at the table, that happens less.

"It is very important that we have women in senior management, both because of their profitability and because they are role models to the young women in the firm," Steve says. "We have 40% women in various capacities throughout the firm. Senior women are showing by example that you can become an owner if you produce."

For example, one woman manages a $1 billion real estate portfo-lio. "She is extremely effective and contributes a great deal to the profitability of the firm," he says.

This was not Steve's first experience with the impact of women in leadership.

When he was partner at RReef, he convinced the other partners to bring the first woman into their partnership. This was controversial at the time. She was going to be the first female partner, and she was also gay, so it was certainly going to be a change. But he wanted her to join the team because she was talented and a unique manager of people.

"We promoted her, and she went on to become unbelievably suc-cessful and productive," he says. "We eventually had four female partners in the firm."

PETER JOHNSON

Peter Johnson is vice chairman and COO of STACK Media, a multi-platform company dedicated to empowering athletes with training, nutrition, skills and other lifestyle information. Peter says, "In our New York City office, we have two very strong marketing executives who happen to be women, and three experienced salespeople, who happen to be men. These salesmen and female marketing executives work together as a team, pitching and managing business together."

Peter has found that this diverse team encourages better and more creative problem solving. "When women are part of these teams, I've consistently seen that more time is spent looking at issues and chal-lenges differently. This works very, very well in problem solving and in profitability."

Previously, Peter was CEO of sports and entertainment at IMG, the International Management Group, a global sports and media business headquartered in Cleveland.

Peter started in the sports business in 1976. The sports industry has always been and continues to be dominated by men. It's still pretty much an old boys' club. In professional football, basketball, baseball and hockey, every team owner is a man, every team presi-dent is a man and every team GM is a man.

When Peter was at IMG in 2006, the company had 3,000 employees worldwide. The highest-ranking female in the company and the only woman on IMG's seven-person management board was Stephanie Tolleson. Stephanie came to IMG having played on the professional tennis tour. She leveraged her relationships from her playing days and worked hard to become IMG's expert on the business of tennis. She diversified her business experience by working on client recruiting and management, event production, sales, consulting, corporate representation and other areas, rather than just specializing in tennis.

> "When women are part of these teams, I've consistently seen that more time is spent looking at issues and challenges differently. This works very, very well in problem solving and in profitability."
> —Peter Johnson

"This later positioned Stephanie well," Peter says. "as she could bring authentic leadership advice to all areas of the business. She coupled her deep knowledge of the sport with a reputation for being highly competitive, but fair. And she earned the respect of her male counterparts."

IMG President Bob Kain, who had managed both the men's and women's worldwide tennis business, moved Stephanie into leadership in recognition of the work she had done. He was also Stephanie's mentor—a tremendous asset for any woman in a company. Having played sports, Stephanie understood competition, hard work, the value of a team and what it meant to win and lose. The corporate culture at IMG allowed hardworking, entrepreneurial, ambitious team players to succeed, and Stephanie was in a division where the management respected those characteristics without consideration of gender. Stephanie went on to negotiate the largest contract ever for women's sports, Sony Ericsson's $88 million title sponsorship of the WTA Tour.

STEPHANIE TOLLESON

Stephanie Tolleson is a shining example of a highly successful woman in the male-dominated field of sports. She was a senior corporate vice president of IMG. She headed the women's and men's worldwide tennis division. In 2005, *Sports Business Journal* named her number four on their list of the Most Influential Women in Sports Business. She personally managed four players ranked number one in the world, including Serena and Venus Williams, Monica Seles and Arantxa Sanchez Vicario.

Before Stephanie started working in the male-dominated business of sports, she was a professional tennis player on the world circuit. Playing sports at a competitive level taught Stephanie life lessons that have served her well in the business world. Learning how to function as part of a team, building a strong work ethic, establishing goals and strategies to achieve them, self-advocating, taking responsibility and making decisions, building self-confidence and experiencing the highs and lows that come with competition are all invaluable lessons that translate directly into the business world.

"To me, it's no surprise to learn that 80% of female executives at Fortune 500 companies self-identify as tomboys or jocks, having played sports at some point in their lives," she says. "Their experience positioned them beautifully for leadership roles in business."

> **"Women should generate revenue and help grow the business to reveal their leadership skills and potential."**
> **—Stephanie Tolleson**

Ultimately, the people occupying C-suites in companies are those with a broad understanding of the overall business, those who generate the revenue, those who have built critical segments of the business and those who are managing the finances. Stephanie says, "Women should generate revenue and help grow the business to reveal their leadership skills and potential. Even the men who don't understand the importance of having men and women together at the leadership table cannot ignore those who help their business expand."

This advice comes from her personal experience. "My simple strategy was always to work harder and better than the next guy," she says. "Don't wait for someone else to give you a to-do list or tell you the next step. Deliver more than you've been assigned. Pay attention, initiate ideas, identify challenges and offer solutions. Be recognized as a problem solver. Create and grab opportunities. Raise your hand, excel, stand out, don't whine."

Stephanie believes that women should not be solely in leadership roles in areas of business that are relationship-centric. Because women bring a number of beneficial "soft" skills to the workplace, they are often overlooked for leadership positions in other areas such as sales and finance. "I think this is a big mistake," she says. "I believe women need to do a better job positioning themselves for these roles and confidently pursuing them."

"Women need to be encouraged to study finance even if they aren't interested in the financial sector," Stephanie says. "You aren't going to make it to the senior management team or the boardroom if you don't understand the financial underpinnings of business."

GRANT DAVIES

Grant Davies is the founder of Davies Consulting, an international strategy and management consulting firm for leading companies in the energy industry. He has been working with talented women since the 1970s, when he first began recruiting women. Prior to forming Davies Consulting, Grant was a management consulting partner at Robert H. Shaffer & Associates and a partner at Touche Ross, now better known as Deloitte, where he managed the company's global telecommunications practice.

When Grant was a partner at Deloitte in the early '70s it was an all-male organization. In 1976, while Grant was interviewing prospective candidates on campuses, he noticed that the women he spoke with were highly intelligent and creative. So he began deliberately recruiting women to bring them into public accounting.

He had great success selecting and promoting outstanding women, until he recommended a talented female colleague for advancement to a key senior position. She would have been the first woman in leadership in that company. His proposal was not successful—she did not get the promotion she deserved. It was vetoed by the other men in leadership. She became frustrated with the glass ceiling there and left to become a star, an outstanding contributor, at a major utility in Canada.

"That experience helped shape my belief that women in business add a tremendous amount to culture and to the bottom line," Grant says. "Fortunately, one of the other women I brought in later became partner at Deloitte."

Today, some of Grant's most capable, high-producing colleagues are women. "An executive VP at a major U.S. utility is absolutely the best communicator I've ever seen," he says. "She's very focused on getting results, and she's very thoughtful and confident in her own skin."

Many women like her are looking for the path forward. Another highly competent associate of Grant's is a woman who is a Georgetown grad, went to Chicago for her MBA and also went to the London School of Economics. "She can change an organization for the better in a relatively short period of time," he says. "Yet you hear men say, 'She doesn't have the right level of experience.' That's an excuse for not moving her up."

"Like in the NCAA, winning teams attract the best."
—Grant Davies

"We've got to get women on the same scorecard as men," says Grant. "You get what you measure. The truth is, shareholders and employees all benefit when you promote women to leadership. And you will attract other highly competent women to your company that way. Like in the NCAA, winning teams attract the best."

PART II

EMPOWERING WOMEN
IN LEADERSHIP

IN THIS SECTION, WE GAIN INSIGHTS from business leaders who understand the importance of empowering women. Dominic Casserley, CEO of Willis, a major global insurance broker and consultancy, shares his beliefs about how accommodating women and encouraging role modeling is a great way to empower and retain talented employees. We hear from Peter Kelly, chairman and director of the International Foundation for Electoral Systems (IFES), which is doing significant work in women's empowerment all over the world.

Two exceptionally talented women share their experiences in media, writing and publishing stories about women in business. Nicki Gilmour is CEO of Evolved People Media and founder of theglasshammer.com, which publishes a weekly series of informative and helpful articles, most often by or about successful, senior-level women in the financial and high-tech industries. Melissa Anderson, a reporter for the *Financial Times* and former writer and editor for theglasshammer.com, shares her views about how bias and assumptions are holding women back in business.

All of these leaders understand that trusting and empowering our talented women is the best way to reduce turnover and improve our companies.

3

EMPOWERMENT IS KEY

In my experience with business leadership and in my coaching practice, I have found that empowerment is the single most important factor for retaining talented women and balancing leadership. Women work very hard to advance themselves. They have to, for many reasons, especially because family and home responsibilities fall more on women than men. Women strive to succeed in business environments where there are many unfounded perceptions about their limitations in business.

Let's face it, women remain stymied by outdated policies and attitudes favoring men. Many companies talk the talk, but far too few effectively empower women, giving them leadership opportunities, teaching them how to succeed in a male-dominated system, giving them the authority to lead and enabling them to continue to contribute significantly while also fulfilling family and home care needs. This is how we must empower talented women.

> **If we trust our people and empower them to fulfill their responsibilities in the best way they can, using all available technology, they will work hard to live up to our level of trust.**

All people, men and women, want to do well and to be successful. So how do we help them develop to their highest potential and contribute greatly to our companies? Today's technology can help us attract and retain talented and dedicated women and men. It is how successful businesses will thrive. If we trust our people and empower them to fulfill their responsibilities in the best way they can, using all available technology, they will work hard to live up to our level of trust.

A forward-thinking leader understands that the people on his team are individuals with different needs. For example, the needs of families are constantly changing—sick days, snow days, teacher conferences, elderly parents and other unforeseen needs. These situations often cannot be predicted. And too often, good people are forced to leave their companies because their managers don't allow work flexibility, such as working part-time from home. The talent drain in today's business world is significantly hurting our companies financially, yet it is not getting the attention it deserves. Turnover is very expensive, way more than people realize. According to Josh Bersin, principal and founder of Bersin by Deloitte, "The total cost of losing an employee can range from tens of thousands of dollars to 1.5 to two times annual salary."[26]

Empowerment is the real answer. If you get good people, you treat them well and let them contribute in the best ways they can, they will stay and deliver to the highest standard. Here is where senior leadership is crucial: you've got to let your team members know that they are appreciated and valued. You've got to ask them for their ideas and help them succeed. Believe me, they will deliver. Just be clear about expectations and goals and then empower them to work to the best of their ability. There is significant room for improvement in retaining talented women who also have family responsibilities, and the effort will pay off, as the examples here show.

DOMINIC CASSERLEY

Dominic Casserley, CEO of Willis, a major global insurance broker and consultant, is the senior leader of an organization with more than 18,000 employees around the world, as well as an informal coach for a number of women. He explains that for about a decade now, there has been a movement in the U.K., where he maintains his principal office, to mentor women to enhance their readiness for nonexecutive board positions. Perhaps more significantly, he is a member of The 30 Percent Club, a group of chairs and CEOs committed to better gender balance at all levels of their organizations.[27]

Still, Dominic is concerned about the lack of women in senior management, saying that the fact that we have only a small percentage of women in very senior management positions indicates a drain of talent. He argues it is the responsibility of HR and top management to work together to analyze the problem from every angle and to devise actions to retain highly capable women. He encourages every company to aggressively reach out to women who aspire to careers in business, and to empower them to combine their business and personal responsibilities.

Most companies do not have all the programs they need in place to meet women's needs. Therefore many women are choosing parenting over careers. But it is up to the company to offer the leadership positions and support that will attract and retain women. Dominic says that at Willis, for example, many positions, even very senior roles, do not require a great amount of travel. Certainly, there is some travel required, but it is manageable for most. Additionally, if a spouse or partner is transferred by one employer, there could well be an opportunity to transfer the employee to the same city within the Willis network.

> **"It is the responsibility of HR and top management to work together to analyze the problem from every angle and to devise actions to retain highly capable women."**
> **—Dominic Casserley**

Another way to empower women that Dominic suggests is to encourage role modeling, where women who have reached a senior position make themselves available to counsel women coming up behind and alongside them about how to manage their work, family and other priorities. Networking within a company is also very important, according to Dominic. Initially, this may be done early, using support groups, and as these women grow and mature in their careers, networking can answer practical matters about challenges, strategies and possible solutions, and offer encouragement and help, such as maintaining active connections while at home for those pursuing parenthood.

Dominic feels strongly that we must look at a company's recruiting policy. Is it 50% or more female to begin with? What are the percentages after five years? After ten years? Longer? As Dominic says, "More than 50% of the talent is female. Therefore we need to ensure we create the conditions for success for this part of the talent population."

"The business environment is changing as the younger generations progress into senior management positions," Dominic says. "The forty-and thirty-year-olds have been brought up in different environments, having studied in universities with essentially 50/50 male/female populations. These generations expect women to succeed in business. With the next generations, we can expect the opportunities for women to get better and better. We'll continue to hear, perhaps especially from women who advanced in male-dominated environments, about the problems they faced, which were extremely difficult, yet may not be the same problems women face going forward."

Dominic's message to those in senior management positions is to help women to have successful business careers. It is in the best interest of our businesses. He believes it's a risky strategy not to have the advantage of the business and leadership skills of half of our population. It's also a very expensive strategy to train and develop good people and then to lose them.

The solution to retaining talent requires a combination of attitude, communication, empowerment, policy and lots of hard work. We can make significant progress if we dedicate ourselves to it.

PETER KELLY

Peter Kelly is another vocal proponent of empowering women. Peter served as national treasurer and national finance chairman of the Democratic Party and was a member of the Democratic National Committee for sixteen years. He was senior political adviser to Al Gore in 1986, 1988 and 2000 and Bill Clinton in 1992 and 1996. Peter was founder, chairman and director of the bi-partisan foundation, the Center for Democracy, from 1984-1997. He currently serves as chairman and a director of International Foundation for Electoral Systems, a bipartisan foundation that works around the world assisting emerging democracies in establishing an electoral process with women's participation. These include Iraq, Afghanistan, Pakistan, Lebanon, Palestinian territories, Egypt, Sudan, Libya and others.

Though the U.S. political arena is evolving as a workplace for women, there is still a woeful minority of women in the House and Senate. However, the influence that women have is growing. During the 2013 fiscal cliff negotiations, while men hurled insults at each other and blocked each other's initiatives, women from both sides of the aisle were quietly meeting for dinners and discussions. It was this group of women who drafted the successful compromise.

Significantly, women are empowering themselves on Capitol Hill. Women like Hillary Clinton and Elizabeth Warren are striding confidently ahead, blazing trails for women who aspire to political leadership. Men need recognize that women have successfully taken on more significant roles in the commercial and governmental world.

Peter Kelly has worked with many organizations where women were appreciated, empowered and advanced on merit, and others where women were suppressed.

"Women are the very core of modern marketing," Peter says. "We need to empower our women so we can take advantage of their insight and skills."

Peter's company, IFES, had a $100 million budget in 2012 to advance women in the home and in public positions. Peter has worked hard on the electoral process in Iraq, where they recently adopted a constitution to move forward with women's participation.

> **"Women are the very core of modern marketing. We need to empower our women so we can take advantage of their insight and skills."**
> **—Peter Kelly**

The experience taught Peter about women's perspectives in elections. "Our experience at IFES is very clear that women are oriented very differently on public policy than men are," he says. "Generally, men look at public policy issues and take a competitive stance. They ask, 'What does this mean to me?' and, 'Can I win?' Women look at the same issue and say, 'How does this affect the children and families?' This is because women are solution seekers. That's why a good deal of our work abroad deals with women empowerment. If women are involved, the outcome will usually be different. When women are involved, they make a huge positive difference in public policy."

NICKI GILMOUR

Nicki Gilmour is the CEO of Evolved People Media, LLC, which includes www.theglasshammer.com and www.evolvedemployer. com. Theglasshammer.com is an online publication dedicated to sharing stories by or about successful, senior-level women in the financial and high-tech industries. Theglasshammer.com is an important resource for women, as well as men, especially in the financial and tech fields. Evolvedemployer.com works with top executives of some leading financial industry companies, helping them create environments in which women are accepted based on their merit, so that they will want to continue their successful careers with their companies.

Nicki has done a great deal for diversity leadership and will continue to do so. Originally motivated to empower women on Wall Street, Nicki quickly realized there was a complex diversity issue with differences of ethnicity and sexual orientation often compounding identities and creating a double-glazed glass ceiling for women. She understands the need for systemic change and wants to help leaders understand what is lost when everyone looks, thinks and acts the same.

Nicki's story is an inspiring one. She moved to the United States in 2004 to launch and run eFinancialCareers, a job board for Wall Street.The impetus for getting involved in gender work began over a coffee with a headhunter who told her that if there was a gap in a woman's resume, he did not consider her for the job. This market disconnect was shocking, and Nicki immediately realized that women were not fully aware of the systemic bias at play. Nicki left the business when it was sold in 2006 and began building theglasshammer.com, immediately convincing journalist friends from around the world to contribute to the site.

"Theglasshammer.com was a mission-driven project for me from the start," she says. "When I was on the Board of eFinancialcareers, I was a young woman from Belfast [Northern Ireland] in a room with old, white, upper-class English men. I felt like an imposter, 'the other,' and so my journey was as much about what I had directly experienced at age thirty-one" and using what she had learned to help others.

Nicki has tackled many difficult subjects in her work to empower diverse women in business. In 2012, she launched LGBT research and had a career event for lesbian investment bankers sponsored by Goldman, PwC, Bank of America and Morgan Stanley.

She hopes to continue this work with a focus on multicultural women in the future. "With theglasshammer.com, we realize that empowerment comes from the interviews we do with senior women," she says. "So we want to keep that going as role models are important. Most companies are still boxing women into confining roles. Women still feel they need to act like men to advance."

She explains that acting contrary to their nature is not a good long-term strategy for women. "Companies don't understand that this, along with systemic bias and barriers, is often why women leave," Nicki explains. "To move things along for women in leadership, we have to acknowledge that policy alone won't do it and that organizational culture is often dictated by leaders but enforced by managers as well as the everyday behaviors of everyone in the company."

> **"We really need leaders of both genders to unpack their assumptions, examine them, and then to decide if these assumptions are consistent with their values."**
> **—Nicki Gilmour**

Networking and support are important ways to empower women to succeed. "Too often, the burden of proof for culture change is placed on the minorities for whom the progress is intended," she says. "So, coalition and support building are essential. When a woman succeeds we want to think that the deal is done; if she can do it, so can others, but sometimes we project our hopes on senior women in leadership who often break the glass ceiling only to fall off the glass cliff."

Though this is a difficult problem, Nicki sees some hope for change. In order for business culture to change, she explains, "We really need leaders of both genders to unpack their assumptions, examine them, and then to decide if these assumptions are consistent with their values. Many male leaders, many with daughters, want to help, yet are not taking the time to understand the complexities that women face. Can men effect change? Yes, they can. Easily? Certainly not easily, but yes, they can."

MELISSA ANDERSON

Melissa Anderson, a reporter for the *Financial Times*, says one of the most important issues here is not so much about women themselves, but a broader discussion about the ways in which bias and assumptions can hold women back.

Melissa explains that these assumptions can keep women from even being considered for a higher position. "Many people—both men and women—just don't see women as leaders, or rather, they automatically think of leaders as men," she says. "It's important to broaden our minds about whom leaders can be. It takes a lot of work and personal and organizational awareness to overcome this obstacle. It has to become natural to recognize and champion folks who show promise, even if they are different."

When the men in senior leadership not only promote promising women, but also pass on to their junior male colleagues that it's the right thing to do, this will change the culture that has long held women back. Certainly, the Millenials and Gen Yers who are experiencing more gender equality will be a huge force in changing culture.

> **"We need leaders who discuss, debate and examine alternatives rather than groups that uniformly decide on a specific course of action without really figuring out if it is the best one."**
> **—Melissa Anderson**

Melissa believes that changing the gender and racial makeup of executive boards will benefit companies in many ways. "When everyone at the table has the same gender, ethnicity, and educational background, they are apt to behave in a pack mentality, and it is less a place for critical thinking," she says. "When everyone at the table is the same, there is more rubber-stamping and groupthink. Long-term thinking is an important issue and is too often missing in corporate deliberations. We need leaders who discuss, debate and examine alternatives rather than groups that uniformly decide on a specific course of action without really figuring out if it is the best one."

With more women at the table, they will communicate and build relationships, Melissa explains, "This naturally contributes to an organizational culture that is close knit and engaged, and focused on the general good of the company rather than short-term, individual gain."

4

RECOGNIZE WOMEN'S LEADERSHIP SKILLS

We know that women's leadership qualities and skills are generally different from men's. We also know that both men and women offer significant strengths. Women are generally collaborative, risk aware, and tend to think long-term. Men are often bold thinkers who take action confidently. Creating a balance between men's and women's leadership styles is absolutely essential if we are going to provide our businesses with the strongest possible leadership going forward. We will do best with a combination of talented and dedicated women and men learning from one another and working collaboratively to create the best and most productive environment for our employees. Certainly, in today's complex and evolving global economy, we need to provide the people of our companies with the most capable leadership we can in order for our companies to thrive well into the future.

In this section, we hear the views of Alexandra Glickman, Norman Barham, Lisa Pence and Meg Boyce Mannion, four very accomplished leaders. Alexandra is a real estate executive who is highly regarded for her intelligence, grit and determination. She is a true go-getter and very comfortable in her own skin. She understands that to be their best, women must be true to themselves.

Norman Barham is a financial services executive who is actively involved with women's advancement. He has great admiration for the numerous talented and highly capable women he has promoted to key leadership positions during his long career. It is Norm's open-mindedness and trusting nature that empowers women to take important steps toward their own success.

Lisa Pence is an accomplished leader in education. As head of the upper school at Holton-Arms, an esteemed all-girls school in the Washington, D.C. area, Lisa is fully dedicated to helping young women develop their leadership and other talents. The motto of Holton-Arms School is, "I will find a way or make one." Lisa instills this drive and leadership confidence in every student. She believes a combination of male and female instruction and leadership conveys the strength and compassion women need to lead.

Meg Boyce Mannion is a consummate professional who demonstrates why women's natural leadership skills are so important. She was one of the first women in an all-male, very conservative commercial real estate company in the 1990s. She succeeded in this difficult environment both by using her technical knowledge, skills and judgment, and equally by being a genuinely caring person.

ALEXANDRA GLICKMAN

As area vice chairman, managing director and practice leader of Arthur J. Gallagher & Co., Alexandra Glickman's expertise is in developing and serving clients who specialize in real estate development, acquisition, advisory, management and all aspects of ownership as well as all asset classes. She has extensive experience in the real estate industry and has pioneered many real estate–specific insurance products and services.

Alex is a driven, focused executive committed to the success of her clients, her company and her team members. She recently celebrated her thirtieth anniversary in the commercial real estate business. In that time she has certainly witnessed the evolution of women in business.

"At first, women gravitated to teaching or nursing," Alex says. "That's where they could always get jobs. Then women began being hired for white-collar jobs: CPA, administrator or attorney. Now insurance has been feminized. It's been a fascinating evolution."

While some women are drawn to risk-averse careers, Alex is risk aware and is certainly not afraid of being rejected. She can walk into any meeting and speak her mind.

Alex tells the story of a corporate meeting in Chicago. There were regional managers, managing directors and others in attendance. She was the only woman. The men gathered there were talking about growth in their most profitable niches, and Alex knew that to achieve their goals, they had to expand training and education.

"One of the guys was off the mark, so I said, 'Come on, guys, we don't have a platform.' I can say that because I have a track record that substantiates what I say. I can run the books. I've earned respect and don't have to worry about offending these guys."

That said, sometimes when a woman gets mad, a man gets nervous. Either that or he dismisses it as being emotional. Women can be very powerful if they direct their energy at something that needs to be fixed.

> **"If Wall Street wants growth, and not off the backs of a few people, we all have to share knowledge. Don't keep it contained in the front office."**
> **—Alex Glickman**

Alex says that being successful is about judging all that gets thrown at you and not losing your head. "It's knowing how to make things work in some logical order. You just have to know your capabilities," she says.

"Some people feel there can only be one successful chick," Alex says. "So they guard their status. But the most successful women are those who are inclusive, those who want everyone to be successful. Women by nature want to be inclusive. They aren't insecure and afraid when someone else does well."

Wall Street is lagging, and women can turn that around. "If Wall Street wants growth," Alex says, "and not off the backs of a few people, we all have to share knowledge. Don't keep it contained in the front office."

NORMAN BARHAM

Norman Barham served as president and vice chairman of global operations at Marsh & McLennan, a leading global insurance broker and risk adviser. Prior to joining Marsh, Norm was president of Johnson & Higgins. He is now a director at Endurance Specialty

Holdings and Endurance Specialty Insurance, and also serves on the boards of Queens College, GAB Robbins, NYC Outward Bound and Brera and is the chairman and director of Coral Enterprises.

Norm remembers a time when he was particularly impressed with women's leadership. "The most enjoyable office I ever led, the Johnson & Higgins New Jersey office, was large and highly successful, and was 75% women," he says. "Our clients were very appreciative of our service, were very loyal, and results were consistently outstanding. The women's contributions were enormous, even when they needed to leave early to pick up their children from daycare or school. They got the work done, and it was done extremely well. I trusted our people and empowered them to get the job done however they chose to, women and men. I believe they knew and appreciated my level of trust."

Johnson & Higgins isn't the only work environment where Norm has noticed the leadership skills of women. "My experience sitting on the boards of publically owned companies is that women make a very favorable difference, because they come to meetings well prepared and open up the thinking," he says. "They want to make the right decisions based on thoughtful and careful deliberation. I truly believe that women are more inclined to ask questions and to listen carefully, to try to understand how others think and feel. They are more open to discussion than men."

> "Women, please take the time to mentor the women and men coming up behind you. Help them to succeed." — Norman Barham

Another critical difference with women's leadership is that women focus on long-term results and effects, while men seem to be focused on the short term. This is a major concern. Norm explains: "I have the privilege of serving on the boards of Queens College and Outward Bound. The women on these boards are dynamite. In my experience, women discuss sensitive issues that men often shy away from. Over and over, I have seen women ask the tough questions in a straightforward manner, not the 'in-your-face' manner that men often use when they are uncomfortable or feeling insecure. When I served on a board that was all men, it seemed like a fraternity to me. That is dangerous, considering a board's responsibilities and the effects of its decisions on the financial stability of great numbers of people."

When men close a business opportunity, they move on to the next client. Women choose to stay in contact. As we've mentioned before in this book, women's relationship-building skills are vitally important in business. "This has proven true over and over," Norm says. "Women demonstrate care and concern about team members, colleagues and clients. They are not as focused on themselves and their own interests as men can be. Women are inclusive in their leadership, which is an important quality. It matters so much to the people working in a business to feel appreciated, that they matter and their ideas are heard."

Norm also has an eye toward the future with advice for women and men in leadership positions. "Build your bullpen," he says, "especially with high potential women. And women, please take the time to mentor the women and men coming up behind you. Help them to succeed. Businesses must focus on recruiting, mentoring and developing their people, including their up-and-coming young women and men. Encourage them to serve their communities, to socialize actively, if they can, and to be role models and helpful to others."

LISA PENCE

When we're talking about women's leadership skills, it's important to understand how women's leadership develops over time. Lisa Pence is the head of the upper school at Holton-Arms School in Bethesda, Maryland, a private all-girls preparatory school outside Washington, D.C. Lisa has a deep understanding of the natural character, qualities and values of women and girls, and she herself models successful leadership qualities and skills.

Lisa has had a long and varied career in the educational field, including holding several jobs at The Field School in Washington, D.C., as teacher, coach, athletic director and college counselor. From there she went on to two other schools as director of college counseling. Lisa has been the head of the upper school at Holton-Arms for nine years. She is currently working on her masters in executive education.

Lisa values her experience working for various leaders and has learned a lot about women's leadership in the process. "I have worked at four different independent schools, for four female and one male head of school. It has been my experience that women may be more apt to point to rather than ignore a problem," she says. "We take a 'we have to deal with this' approach when we hit a snag. It makes the job harder, but my experience is that women are very honest about what's going on."

Lisa has seen the differences in male and female motivation for many years as an educator, and she has a keen interest in how these differences develop. She shares how these differences affect girls. "From a young age, girls are extrinsically motivated," she says. "They work hard to please their teachers and others. Boys are different; their motivation comes from within, and once it kicks in, it is powerful. Women tend to be more driven and high functioning earlier in their development. Holton-Arms School aspires to and expects that its students aspire to excellence. The school is peopled with women who are extremely dedicated and purposeful."

Lisa says that women in academic leadership are successful because they set a positive example for their students. "To get to a leadership position in an academic institution, you have to be adaptable and willing to take new things on," she says. "Men tend to carry out their tasks directly and with alacrity. If women were to act that way, they might be considered ungenerous. Working at a girls' school, women are expected to display gentility. You have to hold yourself to the highest standards so as to set the best possible example for students—and their parents, so women do the transactional work of the school in a warm, supportive manner."

Though it is absolutely necessary to have women in academic leadership at a girls' school, Lisa says that women alone cannot do the best job. "On our administrative team, we have three division directors, two of whom are men," she says. "Girls need to learn from men as well as women. We intentionally have a significant number of male teachers at Holton."

Working with men and women has provided Lisa insights on how their work styles differ. "I have found that men are like brothers to each other," she said. "Their loyalty is a given. They will forgive and forget, and tend to complete tasks without stewing over them or sweating the details. Women may be more affected by social tension or interpersonal concerns from time to time, but they can also be more flexible and adaptable when it comes to responding to change."

"Combining capable women and men in the leadership of organizations is a significant advantage," Lisa says. "In executive meetings, men seem to be more comfortable making major decisions. Women tend to gather information and input that gives them the confidence they need before making big decisions. Women do collaborate more. Women leaders are always thinking in contingencies, always ready for what the day may bring. Both strategies need to be present in executive meetings."

The leadership lessons Lisa has learned in her career translate well to teaching leadership to girls. "In an all-girls school, leadership lessons are ever present," she says. "Every classmate, every club president is a young woman. There is a wide spread of leadership in class, on the field and in clubs. At Holton, we have begun to emphasize specific leadership skills and themes at each grade level." This focus ranges from communication skills and self-advocacy in the beginning to compassion through service and mutual understanding. According to Lisa, these lessons "will help girls in all grade levels develop and demonstrate life skills of empathy, kindness, integrity, resilience and gratitude."

> **"In an all-girls school, leadership lessons are ever present. Every classmate, every club president is a young woman."**
> **—Lisa Pence**

The leadership skills that girls learn at Holton are only the first step in empowering young women to pursue leadership positions. When they enter the workforce, "men and women need to listen to everyone in the room, not just the first person to speak up," Lisa says. "The quiet, reserved person may be more thoughtful. Always ask women what they think. They may pull together what's been said, or say what's missing in the discussion. Women are not gratuitous in terms of what needs to be added to the conversation. So listen to them."

Lisa also has advice for women based on what she has experienced. "In my career I have been open to new opportunities and have been willing to take on a wide variety of responsibilities," she says. "Rather than plan for any next steps, I have taken things on as they have emerged on the horizon. I think it is important for women to have a clear ambition and goals. I have tended to work to the best of my abilities in the present rather than plan for the future. In retrospect, setting goals for myself and working to achieve them would have helped me see myself in the roles I have filled before taking them on. If you can see yourself in the roles you aspire to, you will, if only subconsciously, be preparing yourself mentally for the challenges that lie ahead."

MEG BOYCE MANNION

Meg Boyce Mannion is regional director of brand development at CBL & Associates Properties, Inc. Meg has been in the commercial real estate business for twenty years, starting as a suburban office specialist for Colliers Turley Martin Tucker. Within her first three years, she successfully completed eighty-three transactions worth almost $25 million. Prior to joining Grubb & Ellis Gundaker Commercial, Meg was the office leasing manager for Paramount Group. She was primarily responsible for establishing the marketing, leasing and management program for the Northwest Plaza Office Tower, directly resulting in an occupancy increase of over 23%.

Meg is a quintessential example of the great value of emotional intelligence. In addition to being highly intelligent and knowledgeable, she places great value on relationships founded on trust and respect. She is truly interested in others, personally as well as professionally, which has contributed significantly to her level of career satisfaction and her performance.

Meg was one of the first women in an all-male, very conservative commercial real estate company in the 1990s. At that time almost all companies in the industry were like that: the senior people were all men, and the rules and expectations were set by them. What worked for Meg was to learn what success looked like in the firm and to try her best to deliver to that standard.

Meg learned firsthand how to combine career and family. When she was pregnant, she was in the middle of a complicated lease agreement of an office building. No one in her office was as familiar with the details as she was. Her boss had questions, so he called her in the hospital just after she gave birth. "My mother was shocked," she says. "But I was the only person in the office who handled leases at that point. So I asked her to please give me the phone and leave the room. I gave him what he needed in a five-minute conversation."

While this example may seem extreme, it is important to note that each individual needs to find her own balance. For Meg, this kind of multitasking allowed her to work and raise a family. As she says, "I work best when there's a lot going on. I prioritize well. You don't always get to hold out for the best job. You've got to have a sense of humor. If you have a crazy co-worker, deal with it. Get the work done."

At this point in her career, Meg's kids are in college. She knows many women who have been home for twenty years raising a family. "We're a mother's club," she says. "We have valuable skills. Frankly, we're done with maternity leave. We need jobs. We're putting kids through college. We are very serious and committed long term."

> **"My advice for women is to ask, 'What do you need from me? Let me share with you what I need from you.'"**
> **—Meg Boyce Mannion**

This is a big advantage women have. Working mothers are highly capable people who can bring significant value. Women need to recognize this. With this confidence, they can drive their careers. "Many of us are extremely well organized." Meg says. "We can multitask. We can work together in harmony, we just get it done. My advice for women is to ask, 'What do you need from me? Let me share with you what I need from you. What does good communication look like between us? What is the ideal picture of success?' And then listen. Listening is very important. You've got to digest information before jumping in to make assumptions or comments. Sit back and observe before speaking up."

Meg's ability to communicate clearly and confidently and her tenacious work ethic are extremely valuable skills that create strong and trusting internal relationships. "My first boss had three daughters," she says. "He took me with him, door to door on cold calls. He was a wonderful mentor. My next boss didn't understand part of what I did. He let me roll with it. He's the one who called me in the hospital to explain leasing to him."

After she had children, an understanding boss and a creative arrangement helped her balance. "After I had kids, my next boss let me work at home," she says. "I brought in a female partner who was even better than I was. We created a job share. It was unusual at the time. The way it worked, the boss or my coworkers could call me anytime. I would always be available to help. That is important. It comes with the territory of flexibility, I feel. If they can't get a hold of you, that system fails."

Meg recently made a significant career move at age forty-nine: She started over in a completely unfamiliar field, retail branding. She knew she had to make a change, and here was an industry that was solid and growing. So she reached out to her network and asked questions. This is critical as you make a career transition. Don't be afraid to ask questions.

"Observe, listen, be open," Meg advises. "Look for mentors. Your connections are an invaluable resource for evaluating your career path and new directions. Reach out to people who have been in the workforce a long time, or who have recently changed course. If you've been in the same industry for a long time, touch base with newer colleagues to see how and why they chose a particular industry or company."

That flexibility and willingness to reach out are essential in a career move, and women tend to do this more than men. Meg also has a positive attitude. "I am very grateful that I was able to make a career change at age forty-nine and end up doing something that I really like," she says. "I am also grateful for a stable position with a good employer. And I am thrilled that I have seen my production numbers triple in the past year."

Meg's advice for women is that while you may love your chosen career field, it's wise to keep your options open. No one is immune to economic downturns. You may just want to switch gears, look for a new challenge, more stability or something less stressful. The reasons for moving in a new direction really come down to personal situations and decisions.

"Here's an indispensable tip for making any transition successful," Meg says. "It really helps to have a sense of humor. I've seen some crazy stuff in twenty-five years! There are opportunities out there. By being open to different directions within and outside your industry and by working hard, getting the job done well, and without drama and intrigue, you can be successful."

5

HOW TO DIVERSIFY LEADERSHIP

The ethnic and gender percentages in the workplace are rapidly changing, and so must our leadership. Today's business world is hypercompetitive and will only become more so. We need to give our employees the very best leadership we can, leadership that reflects the population of this country, our team members and our clients. The most effective leadership teams combine talented people whose qualities and skills complement one another, regardless of gender and race. Diverse leadership helps bring out the best in our team members.

As the U.S. population rapidly changes, so must our attitude. The Millennials will comprise 40% of our workforce in just a few years. They have grown up studying alongside very bright and talented friends of African, Asian, Indian, Hispanic, European and other backgrounds. Millennials understand that their friends of different gender and ethnic heritage will make enormous leadership contributions in business. And they will not be satisfied with the status quo, nor with anything less than forward-thinking leadership.

To stay current and attract talent going forward, executives must have the humility and inner confidence to respect and work effectively with people who differ from them. They must promote the best of the best regardless of gender or race. They must promote balance by asking what people need to continue their careers while maintaining rewarding personal lives.

In this chapter we hear from leaders who understand the importance of diversification. They include: Cari Sisserson, executive director of learning and development with Catalina Marketing; David

Thomas, dean of the McDonough School of Business at Georgetown University; Patrick Gallagher, executive VP of marketing of the Super Bowl 50 Host Committee; Mike Crowley, president and co-COO of Markel, a Richmond-based NYSE holding company; Robert Nolan, managing partner at Halyard Capital in New York City; and Lulu Gonella, principal at LWG Consulting.

> **To stay current and attract talent going forward, executives must have the humility and inner confidence to respect and work effectively with people who differ from them.**

Cari Sisserson is an exceptional organizational development professional. She is sensitive, open-minded, caring and eager to help others succeed and learn. Her mission is to help the people of an organization thrive, and to help the organization itself achieve winning results.

David Thomas is an inspiring leader at the McDonough School of Business at Georgetown University. David is renowned for studies and research in the area of diversified leadership.

Pat Gallagher has enjoyed great success throughout a career with the San Francisco Giants baseball organization and now with the Super Bowl 50 Host Committee. Pat knows how to help team members combine their varied skills to perform their best as a team.

Mike Crowley is president and co-COO of Markel Corporation, a holding company listed on the NYSE and based in Richmond. Mike's success is largely due to his equal regard for everyone, learning what is best for everyone and how he can help everyone. He embodies the quiet confidence and humility so important to forging a diverse group into an effective team.

Robert Nolan is the managing partner of Halyard Capital, a private equity firm in New York City. Bob chairs the firm's investment committee, managing funds totaling approximately $600 million. He represents Halyard on the boards of directors of numerous privately owned companies, including The Women's Marketing Group.

Lulu Gonella is a highly effective human resources specialist. In the 1980s, she was part of a pilot mentor program called Career Watch that greatly influenced the careers of talented women who might otherwise have been overlooked for promotion. In her practice today she strongly advocates for mentoring programs such as this because she believes they are invaluable in creating effective team leaders of tomorrow.

As you read this chapter, please keep in mind that when we discuss and implement diversity policies, we need to ask ourselves what successful diversity looks like. We need to consult with our people and build solid policies that allow our companies to benefit from the fresh perspectives and innovative thinking that gender and ethnic diversity will bring. Realize that we need the strongest leadership possible to succeed in ever-more-challenging business environments.

CARI SISSERSON

Cari Sisserson, executive director of learning and development with Catalina Marketing, discovered in graduate school that diversity is a difficult aspect of corporate life, and that few organizations have systemically successful programs. This led her to consider two core questions: how can an organization move beyond assimilation into true diversity, and what is it that diverse people really want and need?

These questions speak to the "now what" stage of diversity policy development that stalls so many organizations. We've all seen affirmative action, desegregation, Title IX and many other federal policies tackle these issues within our communities and schools with varying degrees of success and no shortage of controversies and lawsuits. Many leaders try to have the conversation, and diligently try to implement diversity and inclusion groups, yet most end up frustrated and directionless. Why is it so hard to move beyond an old-fashioned idea, and why is diversity such a difficult topic?

"Thankfully," Cari says, "leadership and language are starting to turn from assimilation to inclusion—a huge first step. Assimilation means, 'If I look like you, act like you, and behave within the constructs of what's already established, then I will be accepted.' "

Assimilation was the way of the '70s and '80s. Many trailblazing women entered into management this way: they emulated men. They toned down emotions, struggled to put in as much or more time as their male colleagues and competed against each other for executive positions.

"Remember the 1980s business suits women wore? These trail-blazing women dressed like men in dark, box-cut suits, without a hint of femininity," Cari recalls.

In those early days many women had the opinion that it was difficult to have female bosses, often saying it was just easier to work for men. There were so few options for women's advancement that the women who made it tended to protect their turf. Work was a place to go, check your emotions and your personality at the door, and act like everyone else—the majority of whom were and still are men.

The predominant thinking of the time was sexist. Men who were firm and aggressive were "strong, decisive leaders," while women with similar traits were "bitchy and frigid." Men who left early for their kid's soccer games were considered engaged fathers, while women who left early weren't carrying their weight. Over and over, men and women were held to differing standards.

"Thankfully," Cari says, "assimilation is no longer the norm, and there are many excellent women in leadership roles. One arena that is becoming difficult to navigate, however, is primary breadwinner status. It's a fact that more and more women are the breadwinners of their families, or for themselves. Being the financial and the emotional strength for a family poses a challenging juxtaposition."

Cari has a telling story to share. She was once a part of a team where everyone, including the leader, was either the main breadwinner or single. Their leader was an accomplished woman. There were eight people on her team—two men and six women, five of whom were executives.

"We were all able to be ourselves and to bring in our emotive states in a way that was both accepting and liberating," Cari says. "Unfortunately, our female team leader chose to leave the organization after an executive leadership change." After that, the team struggled through change after change until three of them were let go, one left, and another was demoted. The remaining team members kept plugging along in discouragement.

"At one point," Cari says, "the three of us had a conversation about how worried we were about losing our jobs as primary breadwinners, and how the stress was getting the better of us. We discussed how different it was for men who, when faced with similar situations, dig in and find their fight mode. For us, the emotional impact of the stress and the fact that we were unable to talk our way through it with the new leadership caused an extremely promising group of female executives to disband."

Cari's experience demonstrates that "going along to get along" doesn't advance gender diversity in the workplace. Including and advancing women as women, respecting their different talents and perspectives, is what works.

Executives often ask Cari what they can do to attract, promote and retain women. This is a process that often requires major policy shifts. Many companies have flextime, although percentages of organizations that actually use or encourage it are rare.

"There are specific actions that organizations should take to embrace such a shift," Cari advises. "First, allow time for the conversation, which conveys your support for women. Next, create opportunities to balance work and family, as women will probably have the main childrearing responsibilities in addition to their job responsibilities. Flextime is key. Finally, build social capital for women through male mentors who can provide links to advancement as well as to female mentors who can act as role models."

Cari has another helpful story. At a conference on employee engagement, she was fascinated by a speaker from a large U.S.-based international company who asked audience members to think about their college days. He had them recall the transition from the structure of high school and living at home to the refreshing freedom of college life. Suddenly, you could choose your schedule, and overnight you were put in charge of your own "performance metrics." It didn't matter whether you skipped or attended classes. What mattered was your performance.

"You were expected to meet the criteria put forth by the professor at the beginning of the semester. Behavior had a direct correlation to results," says Cari. "Then when you graduated and entered the workforce, you were back to having set hours, and limited time off. You were even told what to wear to work. And we wonder why corporations struggle with creativity and innovation!"

A major idea that grew out of that conference was to cultivate that kind of initial freedom offered by college in the workplace. Conference attendees heard proposals such as an 80% remote-work strategy, with regional hubs around the world for meetings and collaboration. Someone in the audience asked how they could tell whether an employee was performing. "How do we know they're performing today?" was the speaker's simple response.

"To me," Cari says, "the idea of managing by time clocks and office hours is so very limiting, especially to women trying to juggle families, work, health, social life and downtime. It makes far more sense to set expectations and measure performance based upon them. Check in with employees quarterly at a minimum, specifically on their performance and progress. Help prioritize and coach before there is a problem. And, depending upon the position, let them manage themselves. Treat them like the adults they are."

Let's realize that when we say we have a mentoring program, or allow a few minutes more for a conversation about diversity, that's really just the beginning. What will make these policies stick is the way that we actually adopt these ideas.

As Cari says, "When coaching a leader, the most important influencer for motivating people is authenticity." If an organization offers flextime, yet the culture doesn't support it, the initiative fails. When bosses wander the floor wondering aloud where people are, and team members look at their watches as you walk in, the pressure to go back to 9-5 is too strong for most to take advantage of work-life balance programs.

> **"The idea of managing by time clocks and office hours is so very limiting, especially to women trying to juggle families, work, health, social life and downtime. It makes far more sense to set expectations and measure performance based upon them."**
> **—Cari Sisserson**

"For some, saying 'work-life balance' with a smirk and an eye roll is enough to kill the intent all together," Cari says.

"Courageous leaders stand behind these initiatives and support them authentically. If we promote a woman to a leadership role without supporting her, we are saying we expect you to assimilate into the dominant male culture."

On the other hand, leaders who not only support but also take advantage of flexible policies can greatly improve culture. One organization Cari worked for, which consistently ranked in the top 100 places for working women, had several female VPs who worked part time. "And they really did work part time!" Cari says. "Their teams respected them, the organization supported them, and they thrived in all aspects of their lives. This is courageous leadership. The question is, how many businesses are willing to take this next crucial step toward true acceptance and integration of women in our workplaces?"

DAVID A. THOMAS

David A. Thomas, PhD, dean of McDonough School of Business at Georgetown University, is a recognized thought leader in organizational behavior and strategic human resource management. His research focuses on issues related to executive development, cultural diversity in organizations, leadership and organizational change. David has coauthored two books and more than sixty case studies and articles for leading academic journals and practitioner publications.

Before coming to Georgetown, David directed Harvard Business School's organizational behavior unit. He also served as senior associate dean and director of faculty recruitment at Harvard; led its business school's required first-year MBA course, Leadership and Organizational Behavior; and held the position of faculty chair for several executive education programs. Before that, he was an assistant professor of management at the Wharton School of Finance at the University of Pennsylvania.

David found the business school to be territorial when he came to Georgetown in 2009. Each department had its own admissions department. Faculty members were not communicating and collaborating across departments to maximize effectiveness. "We had good people doing fine work, but everyone was doing their own thing," he says.

So, based on his experience at Harvard and Wharton, David said,

"We can't operate like this." Slowly, he effected changes. As he and his colleagues implemented these changes, David was struck by the ease with which female leadership worked across silos and created a new culture that had never existed there before.

"My experience in other work settings, which have been more male dominated, is that trying to get people to work across silos is met with more resistance," David says. "Men tend to focus more on what they individually lose rather than what we as a unit gain. Clearly, the women I have worked with here have had a very positive influence on our organizational culture and spirit."

David's experience at Georgetown is an excellent example of the importance of a gender-diversified, high-quality leadership team. Time and time again, it's women who interact with others and really listen to what is being said. David observes that this may be a result of women being minorities in meeting rooms for a long time—they have learned how to make people feel comfortable with them.

"Women effectively put people at ease, and they listen in a way that reflects what a person has said," he says. "Patient listening is an essential leadership skill, not just for what is learned, but also for the way it is appreciated by your team members. They feel valued."

> "Patient listening is an essential leadership skill, not just for what is learned, but also for the way it is appreciated by your team members. They feel valued."
> —David Thomas

He also finds that women are excellent long-term thinkers. This quality, along with effective listening skills, can make a significant difference in an organization. David has a great story to illustrate this point. A few years ago, the university announced a salary freeze to manage shortfalls. To explain this to their people, leadership decided to hold town hall meetings at the business school.

"Before I went in to my meeting," David says, "my operating committee, mostly women, told me, 'What you have to do is assure people you genuinely care about them—that is more important than the facts.'" David says he is glad he followed their advice. "Our female leaders were able to come up with the things that matter to people besides money. The meeting went well, and people on the team felt appreciated. This speaks to women's great capacity for empathy."

Stories like this show what diversified leadership can contribute to the workplace. In order for this to work, David advises women coming up not to lose sight of the way in which their style and values differ from the predominantly male culture.

"Those differences are uniquely your strengths," David asserts. "To adopt a male style would be to the detriment of your individual strengths. And please do not be afraid to be ambitious. I see a marked difference between males and females early in their careers. Men are more comfortable and socialized to be ambitious than young, high-potential women, although these women have so very much to offer and are every bit as talented."

Dean Thomas advises men in leadership to ask and not assume.

"There's a tendency to make quick decisions about people," he says. "Say I've got an assignment that's open. The person I hire will have to inconvenience themselves. There will be travel, late nights. John quickly pops into my head as someone who could easily take on that schedule. I need to stop, though, and ask Beverly if she would like to take on that assignment."

PATRICK GALLAGHER

Patrick Gallagher was the director of marketing for the San Francisco Giants in 1976. "Back then it was all men running the show," he remembers. "There were no women in sports writing or in the media. When women started in the business, it was a novelty. It was more their looks than what they could bring. Now, of course, women are more involved and very credible. But at first, we were afraid to even let women in the locker room. It was like, 'Oh my God! Those guys are animals down there!' We said, 'You guys have to wear towels.' Women who braved that scene were pioneers. They paved the way for all other women sports writers and announcers."

In Pat's experience, his organizations have needed and benefited from women's excellent problem-solving skills, both in management and even on the field, where there are now are female umpires. He has helped develop a culture in which women in baseball have made important contributions.

Pat talks about a VP of communications who is involved in every top-level meeting. "She's a working mom. It's a challenge for her to be a high-level executive and raise a family. At the toughest moments, she and women like her could feel like they're failing at everything. But to lead a full life, to be able to contribute as they can and should, such women need companies open to finding the best way to get the job done."

According to Pat, in Major League Baseball, unless you're an owner, you're a stagehand. "We put the show on every year," he says. "Sometimes it's good, sometimes it sucks. A Broadway play, when it sucks you shut it down. But this is baseball. You just go through the season as best you can."

He was VP of business operations at Candlestick Park when they were having inconsistent attendance. "You've got to have a sense of humor about this stuff," Pat says. "We had promotions to get attendance up."

One contest was for a new PA announcer. "If you think about it, a PA announcer touches everyone who goes to a game," he says. "A good PA, you don't really notice. We had new ownership of the team, so we were trying to improve, make some noise."

Out of the four hundred people who showed up to try out for the job, only one was a woman. When the judges narrowed it down, she was in the top three. "There was something about her voice and the way she announced," Pat says. "She was a huge fan, and she showed you could be a student of the game. She became an instant celebrity. She brought a lot of attention. Over time, she got mixed reviews. We replaced her with another woman. We found someone who was a radio personality. She remains the PA for the Giants today. She has her own style and flair. She created the space. It just seems very natural. She is part of the Giants culture."

The Giants have a wonderful new ballpark now, and the role of women is still important. "They're far more effective," Pat says. "They've got more empathy; they're willing to listen. In the business of sports, women feel they have to be way better than men. They're more buttoned up, professional."

Pat mentions that they had an intern, a journalism student, who was press secretary to the mayor. She got involved in the campaign to build a new ballpark. "She was a real problem solver," he says. "We always wanted to have her in the room. She had her wits about her. She had real confidence. She wasn't afraid to be wrong. She was collaborative. She was also a mother. Trying to do it all and smile wasn't easy, so she got another woman with similar skills to share her job. The women working together made it work. This wasn't a problem for us; it was a great solution."

> **"If you're as smart as you think you are, and you don't include women in the leadership of your organization, you're not as good as you think you are."**
> **—Pat Gallagher**

The half-dozen women Pat had the chance to hire or promote have made a difference. They aspired to the best qualities and character of those who have the most respect in the organization. "Women have played a big part in the success of the Giants organization," Pat says. "With Major League Baseball, you're in the community. People expect you to be better because of how emotionally charged they all are in the community."

Pat continues to coach young people trying to advance. He encourages them to keep their confidence up. He points out that women can be more sensitive than men when dealing with difficult times or rejection. "We're all trying to achieve success as a team. It's not personal; we're not doing anyone any favors; it's business!"

Pat also has some advice for men: "If you're as smart as you think you are, and you don't include women in the leadership of your organization, you're not as good as you think you are."

MIKE CROWLEY

Mike Crowley is another progressive leader. At Markel, there is a female CFO; two of five regional presidents are women; the head of HR is a woman; and several of their top producers are women. How is this diverse leadership impacting the culture there?

"Women create a different tone in strategy sessions," Mike says. "Based on my personal observations, people tend to stay focused in executive meetings with women because that quality of attention conveys that it's no longer a boys' club. Women keep the discussion very professional, and this has a positive effect on the way people interact. Women also generate broader discussion on an array of issues not brought up by men."

Mike tells a story to illustrate. When Markel's five regional presidents get together, the women presidents change the perspective. "They certainly multitask better than many men," he says, "and they bring to light workplace issues that we need to address. We are appreciative of the fact that numerous women and men have two important jobs: the one at the office and the one at home. Their discipline and time management are essential."

Mike says that decision making is often different for men and women and that it is critical to have both men and women in the room. "Where men might make a quicker decision with the macho attitude that if it's the wrong decision, 'we'll just fix it,' women typically don't have that macho attitude and are usually more aware of the secondary or unintended consequences of a decision."

> "Based on my personal observations, people tend to stay focused in executive meetings with women because that quality of attention conveys that it's no longer a boys' club."
> —Mike Crowley

Mike has some advice for men. "Do everything you can to create equal opportunity and eliminate gender bias," he says. "You've got to create the right culture. I have been a big proponent of this for many years. My industry, like others, has been negligent. In fact, a survey by St. Joseph's University shows that in finance, 8.4% of officers are women and only 12.6% of board members are women. We must do a better job. If you don't focus on the opportunity to promote talented women to leadership, then you're limiting yourself to half the population. That's crazy."

While there has been some progress, and more women are filling senior jobs, most are not at the top yet. "Our current CFO is involved in all senior level planning and discussion meetings," Mike says. "She is very impressive in her ability to analyze and direct us to issues that are critically important. We have got to be more proactive in recruiting and promoting women. To be able to recruit talented women, we need to have women in leadership. If there are no women at the top in our organizations, we're going to have a hard time recruiting. The success of women at the top is very visible and inspiring to other aspiring women. So pick the women with talent who have a positive attitude. The visibility of their leadership will demonstrate that this is the way for women to succeed."

ROBERT NOLAN

Bob Nolan is the managing partner at Halyard Capital, a successful private equity firm in New York City. Bob represents Halyard on the boards of numerous privately owned companies. He is a member of the New York and Washington, D.C., bar associations. He also serves as a member of the Georgetown Board of Regents and the Georgetown McDonough School of Business Board of Advisors.

In his thirty-five years working with female business professionals, Bob has observed that the workplace has evolved into a more enlightened state, but definitely has farther to go. "The passage of Title IX did more for women generally than just in the world of sports," he says. "Early barriers have dissolved, and discussion about workplace issues is more candid and healthy. But still, the numbers do not prove out. There is still a low percentage of women in leadership positions in many categories of commerce. Yet the training of female professionals has become better balanced in the financial services industry in my business lifetime, and hopefully this will lead to a more equal distribution of female leaders in the private equity arena as well."

Bob believes that the distinction people often make between women and men in the business world is unnecessary and troubling at times. "Women and men have equal skills in every meaningful category," Bob says. "Both are adept at understanding business models, client needs and customer satisfaction. I work very closely with women in senior management positions who are very comfortable in their roles. I honestly do not see meaningful differences between men and women professionals in my business dealings."

Bob made it a point to encourage female professionals to be an essential part of his business from the start. He has always focused on capability above gender. Halyard Capital owns a company called Women's Marketing. The company is led by two women who oversee a predominantly female workforce. "They set a wonderful example of leadership by mentoring the young female professionals," Bob says. "It is always about having the best people in the room alongside you. Women should play a prominent role in any room that includes the best people."

Bob sees a problem when it comes to work-life balance. "Women are often forced to make decisions regarding balance justification," he says. "I don't believe that reason is the primary issue for a perceived difference between male and female capability. The old boys' club mentality that was in vogue three decades ago is shortsighted and limiting. Thankfully that mentality is in short supply today and has largely evaporated. It remains a reality, however, that hiring practices continue to lack a broad perspective."

Actively cultivating gender and ethnic diversity can help develop a broader perspective for your business. "Business leaders need a broad perspective at the table in discussing various issues," Bob

> "Long live the intrepid souls who value brilliance above all else—ultimately this approach will bring the desired workforce gender balance."
> —Robert Nolan

says. "There are plenty of people who think similarly, but there is a limited supply of those strong enough to think differently in a business setting. More often than not, female executives bring that essential trait. It is true with most elements of life: We need the broadest perspectives possible to succeed in solving business issues."

Bob has some advice for senior executives who make the hiring decisions. "If you don't recognize and embrace a diverse world, then you are doomed to experience success in a limited supply. Today we live in an entrepreneurial world that values talent above all other characteristics. Long live the intrepid souls who value brilliance above all else—ultimately this approach will bring the desired workforce gender balance."

LULU GONELLA

Before starting her private consulting practice, LWG Consulting, Lulu Gonella worked in HR and OD roles at Big Four public accounting firms for two decades. She started part time at Price Waterhouse while earning her master's degree, moved to full time once it was completed, then went on to a small national public accounting firm that merged with Ernst & Young. There, she moved into OD roles, designing and implementing programs to enhance the culture at the firm for twelve years. She then off-boarded to spend more time raising her children.

"By the mid-1990s all the Big Four firms were hiring 50% women, but the vast majority of partners were still men," Lulu says. "We lost women once they got promoted to manager, a process that usually took about five years, because at that point in their lives, women started getting married and having families. Picturing oneself living the life of a public accountant with long hours while raising a family becomes difficult to imagine. Many women believed something had to give, and their career was often what had to 'give.'"

Lulu helped lead a pilot program called Career Watch while she was with Ernst & Young. That program had a tremendous impact throughout the Mid-Atlantic region. It began as a confidential program, about which only a select number of partners and HR people were aware.

> **"It needs to be an expectation in the culture that high-potential women are promoted."**
> **—Lulu Gonella**

"Essentially, we took the roster of women and minorities and selected high performing senior managers—those within three years of potentially being promoted to partner and with high annual performance ratings. We then assigned a senior partner to 'watch' them," Lulu shares. "Watching included reviewing their current and projected client assignments, talking with partners with whom they worked to see how they were developing, and then identifying opportunities for them to get on client assignments that would help them grow. The objective was to quietly work behind the scenes to provide them opportunities to shine. After several years, we decided to take the program out of secrecy and encourage the 'watcher' and 'watchee' to develop a mentoring relationship."

This program led the way for Ernst & Young to develop a global reputation for launching cutting-edge advancement and development programs for women. "Like other mentoring or career development programs," Lulu says, "Career Watch was only as good as the partners who were watchers. Those partners who really embraced their role could make a big difference in their watchee's career. Those partners who did not take much interest in their role had little impact."

Lulu explains that the key was to find partners who really wanted to help others advance. "For programs like Career Watch to work, there needs to be some accountability. Not overly structured, but some sort of reporting back to leadership that demonstrates the quality of efforts and follow-through. Something as simple as having watchers report back quarterly about what they did to advance their watchee's development can be enough."

Lulu says that if an individual approach like Career Watch is to be successful long-term, the organization must also focus on culture change. "Another critical success factor is that top leadership needs to be supporting, talking about and demonstrating commitment to advancement of talented women. They need to hold other leadership team members accountable for doing the same. It needs to be an expectation in the culture that high-potential women are promoted."

Encouragement of mentoring relationships is also important, according to Lulu. "A persistent impediment to women's advancement is the fact that women do not naturally develop mentoring relationships as easily as men do. We've all witnessed time and time again how this happens. A young man just walks right into a senior leader's office, plops down on the sofa and says, 'How about those Redskins last night?' Many women just don't feel that familiarity and ease."

So, how do we address this? What men in leadership need to do more often is reach out to these women, who are busy in their offices getting the job done. Just drop by their offices and chat with them, the same way you do with young men. Invite them for coffee to discuss a project. Or, if inviting one woman to grab a cup of coffee might seem inappropriate, simply invite two women, or a man and a woman.

The key is to create the same opportunities that occur naturally between men, for women too. Women need to take the initiative to build mentoring relationships as well.

6

EXAMPLES OF WOMEN
IN LEADERSHIP

In this chapter, we talk with women who are getting it done. They are working hard to empower women, to make culture changes or simply to be the change, the model of how to advance women to leadership.

We hear from consultants Dana Theus and Diane Tomb; Chair of Willis North America Christine LaSala; Bloomberg Business News Anchor and Reporter Alisa Parenti; and lawyer Sara Steppe, all of whom are out in the field vocally advocating to empower women and to propel women's career advancement.

DANA THEUS

Dana Theus is the CEO of InPower Consulting and InPowerWomen .com, and is a leadership coach and management consultant. Dana specializes in organizational cultures and how to bring out the best in people.

Dana wants to dispel the myth that women don't advance into leadership because they leave the workforce to start families just when they would be advancing to leadership positions. She cites the Population Reference Bureau's evidence of the rising share of women—predominantly mothers with young children—who are working (68% in 2011, compared to 63% in 2005).

"Mothers work, and often pursue entrepreneurship," she says. "They opt to climb the jungle gym instead of the ladder because the traditional ladder to leadership requires that they compromise things they value too dearly, and these values go beyond raising children."

"In order to create business cultures and environments that attract and retain talented women," Dana says, "it is not sufficient to schedule a quarterly speaker to address female employees, or to assume that when family-friendly workplace policies are set, the women's leadership deficit has been adequately addressed. Women and men both appreciate the effort of developing new policies, and both leverage those policies to the best of their ability. But the challenge of women's leadership isn't just about flexibility and time management."

She says that culture change must also occur to truly integrate leadership change. "Women see right through a designated retention strategy if the leadership culture doesn't adjust to welcome and develop women's unique talents and strengths," she says. This is a real problem. Too often, a woman is given a thirty-hour work week, at reduced pay, yet she still believes she has to produce forty plus hours of output. "If her boss is unable or unwilling to coach her into the productive thirty-hour week she's being paid for, why should she believe the company is sincere in its desire to retain and develop her talent?" Dana says.

"The best and the brightest, in particular, feel no loyalty to an organization that does not value them as much as these women value themselves," Dana observes. "In fact, some workplace flexibility policies actually penalize women for pursuing leadership positions."

Here Dana shares a story about how one family-flexibility policy looks to a successful woman. Sandra is a senior manager with a major corporation that she believes does good work. She has a ten-year-old daughter. Because she manages a team, she's not allowed work-at-home flexibility on a regular basis (which her staff members enjoy), and she spends over an hour a day in commuter traffic that she would like to be able to swap out periodically to help her daughter with her homework. Her boss likes the work she does, but "doesn't have the budget" to explore a creative program she's developed. He isn't interested in finding success outside the metrics that their program area has been evaluated on for the last five years. Feeling underappreciated for her creative spirit and penalized for her leadership ability, Sandra is saving her money and is planning to use her niche functional expertise to help other companies as a consultant.

"The opportunity cost of Sandra's departure is more than just the cost of replacing a single employee," Dana says. "It's also the cost of losing Sandra's creativity and enthusiasm to explore new models for managers to incentivize and gain the best from their teams, and from themselves. It's the lost opportunity to evolve and to shape a corporate culture that welcomes and benefits from the skills and talents of women, and the Millennial generation, whose work-life values align with the women who raised them."

Rather than compromise her personal values and sense of self-worth, Sandra will leave and pursue her own vision of success. And Sandra is far from alone. Women are starting their own firms at twice the rate of men, according to an American Express OPEN report in 2013, and over half of the Millennial generation plans to strike out on their own in the years ahead, according to the Deloitte Millennial Research study in 2014.[29]

So how do you keep the Sandras (and their children) contributing to your company?

"First, a CEO must view this challenge as more than a demographic exercise," Dana says. "He or she must have a sincere desire to evolve the company's culture and welcome diverse styles that achieve results. Most importantly, he or she must model this style of inclusive management and require that the leadership culture from the top down welcome diversity of thought and style. This requires personal maturity and the humility to appreciate the abilities of people who are different than you."

> **"A great many companies today have ineffective retention programs because line management is focused on numbers, not people."**
> **—Dana Theus**

"Second," Dana continues, "the company has to talk to its employees and learn to hear not just what they say, but also what they mean. Sandra might articulate her challenge on a survey as a problem with the work-at-home policy that allows her staff more flexibility than she is granted. But spend a little time talking to her and you'll hear her frustration at how her leadership creativity is undervalued and how ineffectively her boss manages her talent."

Once you have a clear idea of the problem, Dana has advice for finding the solution. "Do market research on your employees the way you'd do new product research," she says. "Start with qualitative focus groups and move to quantitative methods. Bring in an outside party and task them with finding what you cannot see. Be open to being surprised by what you learn. Be creative in the solutions you put in place."

You may be surprised by the value that new flexible policies can bring to your organization. "A great many companies today have ineffective retention programs because line management is focused on numbers, not people," Dana says. "Often, beyond the CEO and HR, there is not a solid understanding and appreciation of the benefits that women, Millennials, and other 'nontraditional' employees bring an organization, and the advantages of diverse leadership."

However, don't be discouraged if you don't see the effects right away. "Attitude and intent are far more important than policy," Dana says. "If you sincerely want to retain and promote women and commit to doing so, seek a shift in how your company leads and you will find the way."

ALISA PARENTI

Alisa Parenti is a broadcast reporter who cares deeply about helping others achieve success. Alisa Parenti serves as a Business News Anchor and Reporter at Bloomberg, providing custom live reports for top stations in Chicago, Boston and New York. She has been honored with numerous Dateline Awards from the Society of Professional Journalists and was a recipient of the 2014 Excellence in Financial Journalism Award.

Alisa finds that women make excellent trainers because they lead by example. "Rather than tell you what to do, a woman will walk you through it and watch you do it, to see if you get stuck," she says. "She will dive right in and do the work with you, showing you specifically what is required, and stay with you to make sure you get it. Often a man will say, 'Just do it.'"

However, Alisa says this kind of work ethic can also be a problem for women. "A problem women face in media as in other fields is that we do all the work," Alisa says. "Rather than delegate, women just dive in and do it. The problem with this is that we are considered doers rather than thought leaders. The more we do, and do efficiently and well, the more work we are assigned."

Knowing this, Alisa has changed the way she interacts with senior management. "I work on identifying problems and coming up with solutions," she says. "So when I bring in my project results, I present my company solutions. 'Here's my work, and here's what I think about the problem we're having. We could skip a step here, save time and streamline our operations.' Women need to identify our efficiencies and come to the table with our ideas."

Alisa also advises that women should not try to succeed alone. "You've got to think broadly," she says. "If you develop a small website, you may think it would never be successful if you linked it with a competitor. Why would you do that? Would the *Washington Times* link up with the *Washington Post*? Well, why not? Research shows that linking with competitors gets you more clicks. That connectivity is what can advance your own success. Taking a chance on others' success can draw more success to you."

> **"I work on identifying problems and coming up with solutions. So when I bring in my project results, I present my company solutions. 'Here's my work, and here's what I think about the problem we're having.'"**
> **—Alisa Parenti**

"Without question, I advise women and men in senior leadership to hire and promote more highly capable women," Alisa says. "It will only help their companies. And women have got to think, 'If I do well, it is not at the expense of my coworkers.' I think of my daughter, who was worried what would happen if her friend made the field hockey team and she didn't. I told her that her friend's success does not limit her own success."

Alisa is an excellent example of a female leader who improves every team she is on. "Most women care about their colleagues and want to help them," she says. "They are not driven by their egos and rewards, rather by integrity, being helpful and efficient, and getting things done well with everyone contributing to our success. It's not about me; it's about us."

DIANE TOMB

Diane Tomb is CEO of Tomb & Associates, a full-service public affairs and strategic communications consulting firm. She previously was president and CEO of NAWBO, the National Association of Women Business Owners. Earlier in her career she was assistant secretary at HUD, and also held key positions with Vice President Robert Dole and then-President George H. W. Bush.

Diane has a keen interest in helping women earn the respect and leadership positions they deserve.

When we began our interview for this book, Diane immediately said with great enthusiasm that many people she has worked with over the years do "get it," fully recognizing the special leadership competencies that women bring to organizations. Diane says that she and many of her colleagues have greatly benefited from these mentors who have been excellent role models for others who wish to help women advance to leadership.

Diane gave us these important messages for women in business:

- Do not settle; know your value; boost your inner confidence.

- Do not embody a victim attitude; we're not, and it's limiting.

- Know that so often it's women who get the job done.

- Believe that when we consistently add value, people will stop identifying us as women, rather as highly capable executives and leaders.

- Avoid creating scenarios that make it more difficult for ourselves, such as office politics, personal drama and intrigue.

- Go to our strengths, which are many and very important.

- Keep your negotiating and financial skills honed; they are vital.

- Be genuine and transparent; be comfortable with who you are.

- Realize that women raise moral and ethical issues more than men. If something is not right, we'll raise the issue. Generally, men tend to ignore it.

- Sponsor women coming up behind you. Men are more apt to do this than we are.

- Realize that we need more women role models. Be one.

- Encourage your organization to offer flexibility, support, mentoring, coaching and other professional development so that talented women may be successful and balanced in their lives.

- Make and maintain connections. An active network is crucial.

- Recognize we are great multitaskers. We consistently get the job done.

- Reach out to men and women who have made it; gain their insights. Don't feel you must "stay in your lane."

> **"Reach out to men and women who have made it, gain their insights. Don't feel you must 'stay in your lane.'"**
> **—Diane Tomb**

CHRISTINE LASALA

Now we turn to Christine LaSala, who recently was named chair of Willis, North America. Previously, Chris was president and CEO of WTC Captive Insurance Company, a not-for-profit corporation providing liability insurance to the city of New York and more than 100 private contractors against claims arising from their rescue, recovery and debris removal work at the World Trade Center site in the aftermath of the 9/11 terrorist attack. Chris has led WTC Captive since its creation in 2004.

In agreeing to serve as president of WTC Captive, Chris came out of retirement after a long and successful career as the only female partner at Johnson & Higgins. She was president of Johnson & Higgins New York, president of the firm's tristate operations, and served on its board of directors. Chris was named Woman of the Year by the Association of Professional Insurance Women in 1997 and was a David Rockefeller Fellow in 1994 and 1995.

Chris has seen a lot of change in her career, especially during her time at Johnson & Higgins (J&H). "J&H in the 1970s and early 1980s was male, white and conservative, but with a glimmer of appreciation for people who were smart and worked really hard," she said.

"There were a few men there who were willing to let someone in addition to themselves succeed. This let me build confidence that led me to accomplish a lot. The professional generosity demonstrated early in my career was a touchstone for how I viewed the responsibilities of leadership."

From those views of leadership and comfort in her skill, Chris was able to make some positive changes when she returned to run the New York office after running the New Jersey office. "I returned in the early 1990s to a business office that was deflated. The NY office was demoralized," she says. "There was a revolving door of leadership. People had lost focus and lacked direction. I had to figure out how to make this business unit cohesive. So I communicated, one to one and often one to 100, telling people what was going on and why things needed to change. The five men who preceded me hadn't clarified the urgent need for change. So I explained what we needed to do and why. Hard decisions had to be made, but people understood why they were being made. I told people that we needed to focus rigorously on results, and that their work mattered and their results would be noticeable. Within a relatively short period of time, attitudes changed, and results changed. People could trust and be trusted."

Chris has learned about her personal strengths over the course of her career and has some advice for women working on their own. "Women need to be attuned to and comfortable with their personal strengths and consciously leverage those strengths," she says. "The demonstration of leadership comes from your personal capacity and intelligence that gets honed over time in a genial work environment. Women who are coached and encouraged to express their passions make really good leaders. Women need to value their differences, not conceal them. Sustained and effective leadership is enormously demanding, and I do not believe it can be achieved over time unless it flows from deep confidence in who you are, and well-honed, practiced and deployed strengths."

Openness to trusting and being trusted has enormous sustainable value in the workplace. "In my experience, women are more available, less guarded than men," Chris says. "I think women are more inclined to permit deeper, more personal relationships—this is not about friendship, but rather knowing enough and caring enough to be accessible and approachable. They are more willing to show what matters to them. Women are also more patient. Women know that to get the best out of others, investing time to get to know someone and their full capacity is very important. People will follow someone who is results driven and determined, if that person helps and guides."

Chris says she has always found talented people who have wanted to work for her. "Over time, I have built extensive, multilevel interpersonal connections," she says. "I have always talked face to face with dozens of people, every single day. This is the way I built trust and delivered results, while staying informed and on top of things. Leadership requires an investment of time and personal capital in your team—subordinates and colleagues. If you have the opportunity to lead a small section of a company—a division, branch or product area—you will quickly realize the importance of each individual's contributions, and you will experience the leverage and impact that comes when your team, in fact, believes that everyone matters."

> **"The demonstration of leadership comes from your personal capacity and intelligence that gets honed over time in a genial work environment. Women who are coached and encouraged to express their passions make really good leaders."**
> *—Chris Lasala*

Chris says it is also important to know yourself and where you're really good and keep a little slice with you always. For her it was client work. "I never gave up client work," she says. "I knew I was good at it. Women talk to clients differently than men do. We develop relationships. To have this refuge in your work, where you know you excel, is how you can sustain yourself in your career. There are bumps along the way, and by having a work 'refuge,' you can always have a place to go for reinforcement and sustenance. It's not always, 'what's the next promotion,' it's 'what is sustaining me here and now.' I often retreated to a 'let me work harder and know more' place to help me hold my edge."

SARA REYNOLDS STEPPE

Sara Reynolds Steppe is another strategic thinker and trailblazer. She is a lawyer who decided after experiencing the limitations of working in a big firm that she would partner with women and create a legal culture that worked for families.

Before starting her own firm, Sara was working full time at a big law firm, and then moved to become general counsel of Spieker Properties. After having children, Sara and her partners didn't want to go back to the typical big firm lifestyle of working all day, spending a little time with their kids, and then working until 1 a.m. So they created a different model. Sara and her colleagues Dana Stone and Pamela Lakey started Steppe, Stone, and Lakey (SSL), a full-service real estate law boutique headquartered in San Francisco. SSL Law Firm is now a culturally and gender diverse group that hires strictly for talent and is known for its vibrant culture, responsiveness to clients, and strong results. Most of its partners are women.

SSL stands as a prime example of a smaller firm that enables women to have successful business careers while balancing their personal lives. By placing less emphasis on billable hours and time spent at the office, they attracted the best lawyers from the big firms, all of whom were seeking balance in their lives.

"It simplified things," Sara says. "We could be ourselves. We didn't have to explain where we were going if we left to go to a kid's soccer game or ballet recital. We just did what we needed to do with respect to raising our families. Having primarily female partners helps because things are just understood and don't even need to be discussed. So much can be done online and virtually now, especially with leasing. That made it easier to retain people by allowing them to telecommute if that worked for them, as long as they still got the job done."

Creating more women-owned law firms is an excellent way to close the gender gap in the legal field. Small gender-mixed firms are also well positioned to advance women's careers, as women have more direct access to leadership and clients, and the culture may be less bureaucratic and more open to change.

For those women who are working in more traditional firms, there are some obstacles they can work to overcome. It is often hard for women to negotiate their salary; they don't think to have that conversation. "Male partners tend to look out for each other when it comes to salary discussions, so men don't have to ask themselves," Sara says. "My husband is a partner in a real estate investment firm. He feels that partners need to make sure their other partners are compensated fairly, and that there is an unspoken code that people should not have to ask for themselves, as that might make them look presumptuous. In my experience, that same process doesn't necessarily happen for women. That means that the woman has to be the one to raise the issue during the annual review, which may make us look ungrateful for asking for more money. Women are reticent to ask for salary increases because we place too much emphasis on being liked."

To make matters worse, women put themselves at a disadvantage from the outset. According to *Women Don't Ask: The High Price of Avoiding Negotiation*, a study of 2012 business school graduates, 67% of men tried to negotiate their first salary, and only 16% of women did.[30] That deficit makes it hard, if not impossible, to catch up. "I suspect that the disparity in salaries, in turn, makes retention of women more difficult," she says.

While she says this problem will probably be best fixed by adding more women in leadership, Sara advises women to ask for what they need. "We have to realize that what happens is not a reflection on us personally," she says. "We have to take those difficult steps. When there are more women in leadership, it should help us make more progress toward parity in compensation, provided women are looking out for one another more now—which I do think they are."

> **According to *Women Don't Ask: The High Price of Avoiding Negotiation*, a study of 2012 business school graduates, 67% of men tried to negotiate their first salary, and only 16% of women did.**

To provide an example of how women in leadership can help other women, Sara tells a story about the best legal assistant she ever worked with. "Everything she did was correct the first time," she says. "She was efficient and had a great attitude. Nothing was too big or too small to ask her to do—making her absolutely terrific to work with. She was also very underpaid. And having to ask for an increase was very unpleasant for her. So I went to bat for her. Again, women absolutely have to look out for other women. Hopefully more men will, too. But it can be easier for a woman to have that conversation with another woman."

Sara advises men to get to know and trust their female colleagues in the same way they would with their male coworkers in order to retain the best talent. "Don't forget to ask them to go with the group to lunch or golf," she says. "Women have to have a real reason to stay. It's got to be more than just business. Additionally, just know that any company or firm can handle maternity leave, flextime and tele-commuting. If you have someone working with you that you really don't want to lose, have a conversation about how to make it work. Trust the person. Empower the person."

Sara has always encouraged young women who would like to succeed in business to pursue golf.

Sara also says that male executives need to look out for younger women as well as young men. "Make sure women are treated fairly financially," Sara says. "Think of the cost, from a business perspective. When a woman finds out her pay is unequal, she doesn't feel valued. That woman may leave. There's usually a big cost to losing someone good."

Men also need to know that women want and need appreciation. "It's pretty simple," Sara says. "My boss left a sticky note on my phone that said, 'Good job' when I closed a deal. These small things really make a difference."

Where men can also help is with mentoring. Figure out a way to defuse the awkwardness about going out to lunch, because women aren't comfortable asking. There is something that women can do to bond with male coworkers. Sara has always encouraged young women who would like to succeed in business to pursue golf. "If I could have been a better golfer," she says, "I would have had a way to have more meaningful conversations with men, whether fellow lawyers or potential clients, in a way that was more natural than asking them to have

"Golf can definitely level the playing field—literally and figuratively."
—Sara Steppe

lunch or dinner. On a golf course, you have a different type of conversation than the one you have sitting in the office. The setting is different, it's more relaxed and enjoyable, but it is also over a much longer period of time than lunch or dinner. Obviously, not everyone is going to play golf, but it can definitely level the playing field—literally and figuratively."

PART III

EMOTIONAL INTELLIGENCE MAKES STRONG LEADERS

IN THIS SECTION, WE TALK WITH SUE MAHANOR, Eastern Territory manager at Berkley Life Sciences; and Leslie Smith, senior managing director and head of wealth management at Chevy Chase Trust. Both are exemplary leaders with high EQ who share how emotional intelligence builds strong teams, raises morale and productivity, and creates solid, effectual relationships. Sue Mahanor and Leslie Smith clearly show how women's—and, increasingly, men's—emotional intelligence skills strengthen top leadership.

7

WOMEN IMPROVE MORALE

SUE MAHANOR

Sue Mahanor is Eastern Territory manager at Berkley Life Sciences. She was senior vice president and branch manager with ACE Group for eight years and has twenty-four years of industry experience.

Sue is all about the other person, all about the team. She once said that she feels she should only earn an A as a team leader if everyone on her team also earns an A. She embodies empathy and emotional intelligence, keys to developing strong relationships and raising morale.

"A critical success factor for women's leadership," Sue says, "is our ability to be collaborative. Most would agree that bringing more minds, more opinions and more knowledge to any process results in a better outcome. Women by nature are more apt to collaborate and by extension make sounder and more thoughtful decisions. This has a direct and positive impact on morale."

We're all familiar with command and control leadership. "Men are adept at executing orders and operate well under this approach," Sue says. "Women, generally, want to provide feedback or offer their opinions on strategy, and so we are not as quick to accept 'marching orders.' I once had someone tell me that men are more successful because when given a strategy to execute, they simply say 'got it' and then leave the conversation even if they don't fully understand the strategy, direction or know how to

> **"While some men are naturally sympathetic, women are more apt to take it to the next level."**
> **—Sue Mahanor**

execute. In order to ensure success, women want to have questions answered and costrategize before saying 'got it.'"

While some men are naturally sympathetic, "women are more apt to take it to the next level," Sue says. "Women will have a meaningful conversation with that employee to truly understand how they are feeling and work toward making them comfortable so they can continue to be a productive and contributing member of the team."

For instance, "often managers will be in a situation where one member of a team gets promoted over another," she says. "When that occurs, there are two conversations that need to happen. The first conversation is with the newly promoted individual to congratulate them and let them know that much is expected of them. A good manager will also let the promoted individual know that they are there to support them and help them succeed."

"The second conversation should take place with the individual who did not receive the promotion," Sue says. "Arguably, this is the more important of the two conversations. "Managers who exhibit high EQ and empathy appreciate the importance of this second conversation as well as the need to be proactive about having it. Typically with a male leader, the individual who did not get promoted will have to work up the courage to go to their boss and ask why they were not chosen. Women leaders have already considered the feelings of the nonpromoted individual and make a point to explain thoughtfully and constructively why the decision was made to promote another." This is one of the ways that women's emotional intelligence adds great value to organizational culture and spirit.

LESLIE SMITH

As senior managing director and head of wealth management at Chevy Chase Trust, a privately owned, multigenerational investment management firm, Leslie Smith's leadership team has more than $15 billion in assets under their management and has earned a nearly 100% client and employee retention rate. An attorney, Leslie was formerly a partner at Pillsbury, Winthrop, Shaw Pittman, a law firm with seven hundred attorneys worldwide.

"In my experience, the more collaboration, compassion and sharing of information, the more motivated the workforce," Leslie says.

To achieve this more compassionate workforce, men need to see emotional intelligence as a strength that significantly improves morale and productivity. Men and women just express themselves differently. "The impact and meaning of all communication is in how it is received," Leslie says. "Men are more outward in their expression of anger or frustration, and women are more apt to cry. I'm sure it happens on occasion, but I have never seen a woman explode in the office. I have seen women cry; I have seen women cry when defending their performance or asking for a raise. Men hate it when women cry. They may think it's manipulative. I think it's almost always genuine. It's just harder for women to defend themselves, to promote themselves and sometimes even to talk about themselves."

> **"In my experience, the more collaboration, compassion and sharing of information, the more motivated the workforce."**
> **—Leslie Smith**

"While it may not always be effective to cry or be emotional, particularly in a male-dominated environment," she says, "I worry that women may try to tamp down their emotions and passion to become more like the guys. Making the workforce more homogenous is detrimental, as there is a lot of evidence that diversity of viewpoint leads to better decisions and better results. Morgan Stanley has launched a fund that will invest only in companies that have at least three women directors, believing the fund will out perform."

Leslie says that it is important for women headed for leadership to keep trying. "Do not assume you won't get to the top," she says. "Don't assume it's too hard, either to get there or to do the work when you do. Value your skills and emotional intelligence. I was terrified to join the management committee when I was a young law firm partner many years ago—I didn't think I was ready or that I could hold my own with the senior men on the committee. But I went for it, and I was surprised and relieved to find that it wasn't that hard. Sure, my ideas were often rejected, but I learned a lot and it gave me the experience and confidence to go on to other leadership roles."

8

RELATIONSHIPS MATTER
AS MUCH AS RESULTS

The quality of our internal relationships makes a critical difference in businesses that thrive. The better our relationships with our people, the more we will accomplish. Our people want to do good work and be successful. It is important that they feel that we, their leaders, are helping them. The people doing the work of our companies need to feel appreciated and valued, that they are important members of a team they respect, and that their ideas are heard and matter.

Yes, we are all very busy. In fact, too busy. We must work toward freeing ourselves up so we can have time for conversations, even short conversations. We must minimize our meetings within the C-suite and make time for the people doing the work all around us.

As Susan Scott writes in *Fierce Conversations*, "Conversations are the work of a leader." If we project an attitude of genuinely caring about our team members' ideas and success, and if we reprioritize our time, we can develop quality relationships that improve the spirit of our organization, and drive and sustain superior results.

In this chapter we will hear from leaders who are putting relationships first. Al Ritter, president of Ritter Consulting Group, points out in our discussion that quality relationships are created and maintained with conversations, not with emails, newsletters and conference calls. Diane Trister Dodge, principal of Teaching Strategies, is a former preschool teacher who is a leading voice and visionary in early childhood education. She designs workspaces that promote conversation and collaboration. Betsy Balderston, former principal and senior vice president of Johnson & Higgins, is also a strong proponent of business relationships. Betsy is a strategic project leader and change agent who adds depth to boards with her expertise in organization development, business development and fundraising.

AL RITTER

Al Ritter is president of the Ritter Consulting Group headquartered in Geneva, Illinois, outside Chicago. He has extensive experience in consulting and was previously in senior executive positions with Citigroup, Swift & Company and PepsiCo. Al is the author of two books, *The 100/0 Principle: The Secret of Great Relationships* and *Life Is a Paradox*. A devoted proponent of servant leadership, Al is a terrific source of helpful ideas and inspiration.

One of Al's observations about successful business is that most successful organizations include talented women. "Organizations that consistently generate breakthrough earnings are typically on the cutting edge of talent development," Al says. "They realize they can achieve a distinct competitive advantage by developing a high-performing and diverse workforce—one that includes women in senior leadership positions. They know it's the smart thing to do."

"In my twenty-five years of consulting for thousands of leaders across all industries," he says, "I have learned that women have the uncanny ability to generate measurable results and the equal ability to create relationships. I define leadership as the dual commitment to both results and relationships, never compromising one for the other. Women have the distinct ability to do both."

Why is that important? "Most people don't realize that relationships are the most important factor in achieving success, in business and any other walk in life. Women have a better ability to create relationships and build morale than men do. They bring their hearts to the table and a care and concern for others. In contrast, men tend to emphasize their competence, their credentials. Many men operate a specific way—a single-minded drive for results with too little attention to relationships."

This is a problem that has developed because men are taught to measure success by achievement alone, according to Al. "Many of us men define ourselves by our success while inadvertently diminishing the people around us—through our tendency to display our competency, strength and competitiveness. Few of us men were taught that we could demoralize and defeat others and ourselves and damage results by operating this way. But we are damaging both our relationships and our results with other people. Women, by contrast, tend to express warmth and generosity, and they get the job done."

"Many of us men can't see the importance of relationships. We look at kindness as counterintuitive—the soft, touchy-feely stuff. We view command and control as a tenet of overachieving, especially in tough economic times. However, the truth is the best leaders emphasize the importance of others. They lift others up. They are responsive to their teams' needs so that the company mission, vision and goals are achieved—even in tough economic times."

> "In my twenty-five years of consulting for thousands of leaders across all industries, I have learned that women have the uncanny ability to generate measurable results and the equal ability to create relationships."
> —Al Ritter

Al finds that women are better at being uplifting leaders who create solid relationships. "They are empathic, thoughtful and nurturing," he says. "They are geared to help and care. Women demonstrate their commitment to relationships without compromising their commitment to results."

Working for a small consulting firm in the late '80s, Al first became aware of the power of female leaders. "There were eight or nine consultants, and two were women," he says. "The two women really helped the firm be successful. They established great trust and rapport with clients. A lot of the success we had in that small firm was due to them. A two-month engagement often became a year-long engagement because of their excellent rapport with the firm's clients."

While consulting for Reebok, Al worked with Chief Financial Officer Deb Smith. "Normally, a CFO brings a certain level of fear and intimidation to the room," Al says, but this time that wasn't the case. "She pushed people for results, but with firmness and gentleness. She was about service, support, and competence. The financial results at

Reebok during her ten years of service reflected her terrific leadership qualities."

Al has another story about a woman he met while consulting with a major pharmaceutical company. She was a plant manager named Janet Spear. "Janet is a great leader," he says. "There was something different that I noticed right away when I walked in the room. There was camaraderie. People were smiling, looking at each other in the eye. Janet later told me that they only hire people who give the right answer to this question, 'Do you care about your coworkers as much as you care about your own performance?' Janet's plant is at the very top in all production and safety measures."

In Al's leadership consulting and coaching work, he refers to the best leaders as servant leaders. "Servant leaders seek to grow and develop people as an end goal of equal importance to results. Their behavior combines a drive for achievement while demonstrating emotional intelligence with everyone around them.

"In my experience, more women than men demonstrate servant leadership," Al says. "Traditionally, men have observed and learned that leadership is about ego. We're impatient for results, and less forgiving with our people. The drive for success is a good thing, but when the bottom line is the only goal, that drive can override people. Morale and job satisfaction fall by the wayside. The leader, by relentlessly focusing on results, will often, over time, damage the team's performance."

DIANE TRISTER DODGE

Diane Trister Dodge is the principal of Teaching Strategies, which she founded in 1988. She started out as a preschool teacher who observed firsthand what was needed in the field of early education. Teaching Strategies began in Diane's basement, with a filmstrip and an early edition of The Creative Curriculum—a product that would later become the most widely used preschool curriculum throughout the country.

As an early childhood educator writing materials for teachers and as a business owner of a predominately female company, the concept of emotional intelligence influenced Diane's thinking. Diane observes, "Women tend to have high EQs; it's why we are skilled at building relationships, responsive to our customers and collaborative. It's why women leaders are so successful."

Since Diane's early childhood education publishing company employs mostly women, she says the "business culture is inclusive, collaborative and responsive, which comes naturally to most women. As the Harvard Business School initiative on gender equity pointed out, business school culture needs to change so women's ideas are heard and valued."[31]

Diane says this is a very important finding for her industry. "Confidence begins in early school experiences," she says. "It has been ingrained from a very early age that women's ideas aren't as valuable as men's. It is well documented that teachers focus more attention on boys and are more likely to call on boys, conveying that their ideas are more valued. For this reason, it's very important to create a business culture that emphasizes relationships and empowers people to feel valued."

One of the reasons Teaching Strategies has been successful is that it has formed relationships with active teachers and is very responsive to their needs. Diane says that early childhood educators tell her all the time, "I dream of something I desperately need, and when I turn around, Teaching Strategies has already created it." Now that is really knowing, valuing and respecting your customers.

As long as Diane can remember, she always wanted to be a preschool teacher. After finishing college, her first teaching job was working with three-year-olds at the 92nd Street Y Nursery School in New York City. Later she moved to Mississippi to work on a Head Start program, Diane applied for a job as a teacher in a new program that would serve nine hundred children. The office of economic oppor-

> "It is well documented that teachers focus more attention on boys and are more likely to call on boys, conveying that their ideas are more valued. For this reason, it's very important to create a business culture that emphasizes relationships and empowers people to feel valued."
> —Diane Trister Dodge

tunity that was overseeing the antipoverty program sent a represen-
tative to help the community action group set up the program. To
her surprise Diane was interviewed to be an education coordinator
for the program, not a teacher.

Diane said she had no idea how she was going to do that job. "I
don't know anything about training teachers," she said in the interview. "But the interviewer saw something in me that I didn't see in
myself. The three years that I spent working for this large Head Start
program changed my life. From teaching young children in a class-
room, my work evolved into helping others to gain the knowledge
and skills to teach effectively, and eventually, creating my own publishing company many years later."

Diane says that she would not have made that transition without
supportive mentors, the confidence to take risks and a vision of what
she wanted to accomplish. "Years later, I put those skills to use when
I could not find a publisher to accept my proposals for publishing
materials I developed for teacher training," she says. "I knew that
what I had developed would be helpful to other trainers. So in 1978,
I self-published a filmstrip, and the first edition of The Creative Curriculum was created on a typewriter! I called the filmstrip 'Room
Arrangement as a Teaching Strategy' and pretended there was a publishing company called Teaching Strategies. I developed a brochure
and gave presentations at conferences—and the two products began
to sell, as I knew they would. In 1988, I officially incorporated the
company and began working full time for the business."

Diane has advice for executives who want to run a successful people
business with good EQ. "Leaders need to keep reminding people of the
company's mission, and to build internal relationships continually by
recognizing how each person is contributing to that mission," she says.
"Women are good at acknowledging people in this way. For many
years, I would send out an email to all staff acknowledging each person's anniversary at the company and describing what they do to support our mission. Now that we have grown, our human resources department publishes a quarterly newsletter listing all the staff birthdays
and anniversaries for those months. I still try to write to each person a
brief and personal note on his or her anniversary."

9

TEAM BUILDING IS ESSENTIAL

Leadership means positively influencing others by encouraging and helping them do great work and meet and exceed our collective goals. True leaders encourage team members to work together effectively, to share ideas and collaborate to help serve customers and clients, to grow our businesses, and to have pride in their work and their company. For a company to be successful, we need team members who are happy and who are positive influences on others. Good morale and happy workers create better results. As we've said, it really is all about our relationships with one another. I do not mean we all have to be friends. What I do mean is that there must be an atmosphere of genuine caring and respect.

We need the leaders of our teams, starting with our CEOs, to be forthright and sincere in their messages, to be all about the team, to appreciate and value the people doing the work of their companies, and to want to know their ideas. The best leaders going forward will be servant leaders, those who help their team members succeed, who realize the importance of bottom-up ideas and who share credit. The best leaders are not ego driven. They have the humility and inner confidence to want to help and to see others succeed.

Too often we see people try to get ahead by taking credit for a successful outcome. The leaders profiled in this chapter are the exception. Paige Wisdom, former senior executive at Freddie Mac, and Katia Goforth, vice president of VoIP systems engineering at Mega-Path, choose to shine the light on their teams.

PAIGE WISDOM

Paige Wisdom is former executive vice president and chief enterprise risk officer of Freddie Mac. She was responsible for providing the overall leadership, vision and direction for enterprise risk management and leads an integrated risk management framework for all aspects of risk across the organization.

Prior to joining Freddie Mac, Paige served as a business unit CFO at Bank of America and as the chief financial officer of the corporate bank at Bank One Corporation/J.P. Morgan. Before working at Bank One, Paige held management positions at UBS/Warburg Dillon Read, Citibank Salomon Smith Barney, and Swiss Bank Corporation.

Paige faced a challenge when she came to Freddie Mac: her new division suffered from low morale and was not very effective. "The organizational structure was fragmented," Paige says. "I offered to create a risk business plan for the new CEO, Ed. My business plan focused on how to build an enterprise risk function and set a proactive, frank tone for the company's risk management."

She says the keys to her success are teamwork and good listening. "I am a fact-based decision maker," Paige says, "and I try to be as inclusive as I can and as is appropriate. I try to be a consensus builder. I listen to understand and learn and I am decisive. They are not mutually exclusive. They can go together. I work in partnership with our business units. I try to provide helpful oversight, which will assist our business units in understanding and factoring management of risk."

The first thing Paige did when she got the Freddie Mac was to form focus groups to find out what was wanted and what was needed. "The answer was clear," Paige says. "They wanted to learn and grow. Isn't that the same as in all organizations? So I brought in great talent and focused on two things: diversity of our people and their professional development. It was important to me that I put them in positions to succeed."

She arranged coaching, workshops and brown-bag lunches so people could come together and learn skills. Freddie Mac's risk division had people from different cultures, so Paige's team concentrated on persuasive writing and speaking. "These development opportunities were appreciated and welcomed," Paige says. "We'd explain the importance of clarity." This program was very effective at improving communication.

Paige also noticed that the development path for women at Freddie Mac could use some improvement. "I noticed that because some of the talented women in the organization were excellent organizers," she says, "they were put in project management roles and were not responsible for financial content, resulting in the inability to move up in the organization. So I started the Women's Cohort. Most women have the soft skills, as in high emotional intelligence, which help develop important relationships. I encouraged them to further develop their quantitative skills. We brought in high performers. We had whiteboard meetings, and encouraged open-space thinking. This led to women practically growing in front of me, they were so eager to learn. As we were faced with challenges and problems, I'd present them to our team, and had those highly capable people develop solutions. This skill training and mentoring resulted in the sponsoring of our many high-potential women at Freddie Mac."

When a new CEO recently joined Freddie Mac, he sought feedback of the senior management team. "The feedback about me was, 'People are afraid of her,'" Paige said. "Why, because I'm smart and all about getting things done? All I wanted to do was do my job well and help Freddie Mac succeed. I engaged an executive coach, who helped me learn how to respond to tough situations—to be direct, to call them on what was going on, and in a polite and respectful way. Most of the time it worked."

"What people outside our group of about 700 people may not realize is that my focus is on our people, helping them learn and grow, putting them in a position to succeed—that's how we get things done. I sometimes wonder if others are uncomfortable that a woman is having considerable success. I would hope that is not the case. If we are going to be the successful organization we want to be, women and men must be supportive of one another and work effectively together."

Paige says that is important for women to help other women as well as men who are starting out. She says that she had female mentors who taught her skills and self-confidence. "I had a recent experience where two talented women were initially denied promotion to officer titles," she says. "One was an amazing contributor, but quiet, not enough 'executive presence.' The other was take-charge, yet considered too aggressive. I went to lengths to support these two women. Would their styles have been interpreted in the same way if they were men?"

> **"I want my team members to succeed. I never worry that they will outshine me. I hope they do. I want my team members to enjoy working together."**
> **—Paige Wisdom**

"To me, leadership is about helping people, all of them, to have the inner confidence that they need," Paige says. "I want my team members to succeed. I never worry that they will outshine me. I hope they do. I want my team members to enjoy working together. We are definitely a more effective organization when women and men work well together. Women are not risk averse, but we are risk aware, which is can be a critically important counterbalance."

Paige has an effect on her employees even after they move on to other jobs. "I just received a hand written note from Shari Daw, a senior officer who just moved back to Chicago," she says. "The note read 'Thank you, Paige, for the great experience and fun working together, and for letting me do my job and build my team.' Shari's note is what I hope my leadership is about."

KATIA GOFORTH

Another highly effective team leader is Katia Goforth, vice president of VoIP systems engineering at Mega-Path. Katia is exceptionally intelligent, yet low key. She has the quiet confidence to stand up for her ideas and the right things to do. She achieves great results thanks to her excellent team leadership, and she seeks no credit, just the satisfaction of her team members doing outstanding work and succeeding.

Katia is very appreciative of her team. "My engineers are brilliant," she says. "I don't tell them what to do. Instead I ask them, 'Do you think this is a good idea?' Or I'll say, 'This is the problem I'm trying to solve. What do you think?' I always make sure they feel they're important. I am very proactive and believe proper planning up front will make all projects more successful. There are twenty-five people on my team; three managers and high-level engineers. I've got all A players who have been with me up to fourteen years. They are all very experienced and very knowledgeable."

The emphasis that Katia puts on teamwork has had real value for her organization. "One of the things that makes our team so powerful is the lack of attrition and the intellectual property we have accumulated over the years," Katia says. "When you lose an employee, information just walks out the door and ultimately weakens the team. I like to reward them publicly, by email or gift cards. I proactively reach out to upper management and request that they send emails to my team acknowledging the work that has been done. I have team members in a variety of locations, and we all collaborate and lean on each other so even those that are remote from their leader always feel involved."

One reason Katia's team leadership is so effective is that the people on her team work toward larger goals and a larger purpose in life. "I am a big believer in transparent leadership," she says. "I connect everything my team does to the bottom line." Katia knows that people need to know what success looks like, so she tells them how their projects are affecting the company. She says that this doesn't always happen in companies. "In some corporations, men don't do big-picture thinking, and they keep information to a limited subset of individuals."

Katia understands how employees work and how to leverage her team. "I really enjoy giving my team upward

> **"One of the things that makes our team so powerful is the lack of attrition and the intellectual property we have accumulated over the years."**
> **—Katia Goforth**

visibility," she says. "I get them face time with leadership at every opportunity. I am constantly coaching and developing them to take on more responsibility and handle new or different tasks. It's exciting for me to show them off. I don't feel threatened by doing this because I feel ultimately it strengths the team."

She also gets excited about projects and is happy to share them with her team. "I have fun with my team," she says. "I'll say, 'Can you do this?' And they show me how fast they can do it. So I get to say, 'I'm impressed now.' I genuinely care about my people. I'm loyal to them. They trust me, and I look out for them. They stay with me, and I stay. My connection to them is far more important to me than a larger paycheck elsewhere."

Katia's field, telecommunications, is a very male dominated. "There is one woman in executive leadership at my company," she says. "This woman has been my mentor for the past nine years, and she is very rational and effective. She has helped me tremendously over the years with specific feedback to help me progress my career."

Consistent hard work has been Katia's strategy to advance her career and earn the respect of her peers. She is a consummate professional, as are many hard-working women. She is methodical and makes consistent progress. She says that it is very important to trust your people and teach them the skills they need to succeed. To this end she has taught her team fundamental values and practices, including documentation, standardization and automation.

"I like to make sure we always do things in the same way," she says. "Process and procedures matter in engineering. People then know what to do and how to do it. Over the years I have found that some people will subconsciously withhold certain tasks for job security. I have shown my team that you want to share everything you know because that will ensure that you continue to learn new things and don't get pigeonholed into doing the same things for your entire career."

As a good manager, Katia knows that employees don't leave companies, they leave managers. "The quality of the work environment is so important," she says. "Do they feel appreciated? Do they enjoy working there? Do they enjoy their coworkers? These are all the responsibility of their leader, but often managers think that employee morale is a function of the human resources department."

Katia has some advice for women in leadership. "Work hard but don't overcompensate," she says. "Being tough and treating your people badly does not help our cause. It makes things worse for all of us. And ask for promotions. Until male leaders understand the value women bring to the table, we have to ask for opportunities to advance."

PART IV

WORKING SMART

IT'S ABOUT RESULTS, NOT HOURS

DID YOU KNOW THAT 91% OF HR professionals believe that formal implementation of flexible work arrangements (FWAs) improves morale, and 89% report higher retention?[32] In this section, we discuss how companies can benefit from the growing trend toward FWAs, in which results matter more than hours at a desk in the office. We show how important it is to trust and empower talented women and, increasingly, men who strive for success and fulfillment at work and at home.

I know that many executives believe face time is the only way to secure busines¹s. Certainly, there are crucial meetings and new client contacts that should be face to face. But there are many projects and responsibilities that can be accomplished efficiently away from the office. Many women and, increasingly, men, are high-level producers—on their own schedules.

In fact, a 2013 Catalyst study found that face time does *not* always determine top performance outcomes.[33] And where there is a lack of flexibility, talented women are forced to leave promising careers.[34] Remember, our people are most productive when they are happy.[35]

We hear now from Lizann Rode and Marc Camille, high-performing professionals whose work ethics model what FWA can—and will—accomplish, for all of us.

LIZANN RODE

As executive director of alumni relations at the Wharton School at the University of Pennsylvania, Lizann Rode's primary mission is to support and enhance the engagement of Wharton's 92,000 alumni all over the world. Among Lizann's accomplishments at Wharton, perhaps the most visible has been the expansion of lifelong learning opportunities at alumni events.

After earning her law degree, Lizann joined the law firm of O'Brien and Ryan, where she was named partner in 2005. Prior to joining Wharton in 2012, she served as the director of external relations at the prestigious Springside Chestnut Hill Academy in Philadelphia.

Lizann is championing the life quality issues that now pervade education and business. In his book *Baby Bust: New Choices for Men and Women in Work and Family*, Stew Friedman, founding director of Wharton's Work-Life Integration Project, writes that in 1992, 79% of male and female business school graduates planned to have a family. In 2012, that number dropped to 40%. More women are leaning in to their careers, and men want to be more engaged in fatherhood. But both are experiencing work-life conflict that is making it more difficult to start a family.[36] "Basically, companies are making decisions that are a drain on talent," Lizann says. "Women leave companies because there's too much pressure or they can't meet both career and family or life demands. Interestingly, it is not just children that take women out of the work force. Care of aging parents is a similar time challenge that many professionals have to opt out of work to accomplish for a time. They're not making enough to justify childcare or adult caregiving and all the associated costs."

But Lizann sees a cultural transition occurring in business now that will help create balance in the workplace. "Empathy and warmth are starting to be highly valued," she says. "Women who are exhibiting these traits are getting it done. The research on success is on the whole person now. EQ is seen as relevant. Integrity is being advertised as the desired outcome at universities. The world is becoming more human. Men and women want to work at family-friendly companies."

"Speaking from my point of view as a woman in business, I know that half of the talent pool—women—are not reaching the C-suites," Lizann says. "I practiced law for fifteen years, seven of which were part time until my youngest started kindergarten. I was with a medium-sized law firm that allowed me to construct my own part-time ar-rangement—which ultimately became a model for other women who went part time there. I worked and billed at 60% and came in Monday, Wednesday and Friday. If there was a big meeting on Tuesday, I came in on Tuesday, not Monday. At some law firms you can't do that. Many law firms have a structure you can't deviate from. My firm allowed me to define my role. They made it safe to ask. My end of the bargain, of course, was com-mitting to the many hours I also worked at home to accommodate the demands of the work."

After five years full-time and seven years part time, Lizann made partner. While part time, she had brought in a major client, another first for the firm. After initially wondering how she could manage a client part time, in conjunction with the managing part-ners, Lizann came up with a plan for how she would manage the client relationship and develop a compen-sation plan for that work. "I lobbied hard to manage the relationship," she says, "and because I had brought the client in while working part time, I knew I could manage it part time with the right support."

> "Empathy and warmth are starting to be highly valued. Women who are exhibiting these traits are getting it done. The research on success is on the whole person now. EQ is seen as relevant. Integrity is being advertised as the desired outcome at universities. The world is becoming more human. Men and women want to work at family-friendly companies."
> —Lizann Rode

Lizann says that it was fair that it took longer for her to become partner than some of the men. "While my firm didn't have a specific number of years of a partnership track, there was a male colleague who made partner before I did," she says. "But I had two children and worked part time for seven years. The only way this works is if there is recognition that when you are part time, promotions are going to be commensurate with the work performed.

"There also has to be an understanding that you can't take on every big assignment when you're part time. You just can't. But part time legal work is an arrangement that can be win-win. Women can maintain forward momentum, they don't lose significant time and traction in their career, and law firms don't lose talent. Firms retain the investment they have made in their human capital. Additionally, there is tremendous productivity in the part time work force. Women who work part time bring great focus and efficiency to the job. At one point, when we had four women working part-time, my boss said, 'I'll take a law firm of part timers. You don't waste time. You get it done.' "

Lizann had the opportunity to make a unique career choice. After practicing law, she took a job in external relations at her daughters' school.

"Making a career change can come with great risk for which many don't have the bandwidth or life circumstances to explore. I feel very lucky to have been able to do that. Working at my girls' school provided great opportunities to witness their sports and activities and to be part of their community, and I loved it. It also put me on the platform to make the move to my current role at The Wharton School. And the hidden gem of working in a school is snow days! Not many professions get snow days. It is an opportunity I highly recommend."

In her work at Wharton, Lizann's biggest challenge is time management and prioritizing all of her work. She is responsible for two international conferences a year, one year in Paris and Tokyo. This is just part of her role in leading alumni relations. Lizann has got to keep her eye on the big picture and maintain focus on Wharton's core priorities. So she is reevaluating and expanding staffing according to these priorities. "Our international community is growing," Lizann says, "so my other challenge is, do I travel more? Do I delegate? I have two daughters, so travel is a decision. I have excellent support in that I have a terrific boss and I am part of a great management team, of which three of the five are women. Those of us who travel, including my boss, have families, so there is thoughtful decision making around travel. Family commitments are greatly respected. This position was a big step forward in my career, and there is tremendous opportunity for growth, so I am committed to making it work for our family."

Lizann appreciates her journey when she reflects on all that she has done, but she still sees more work ahead for culture and for herself. "I've had great opportunities, worked hard, and I truly enjoy working and what I do. I delayed my opportunity for partnership when I chose to work part time to be home with my children, with no regrets. And I reached that milestone in a timeframe that was equitable. As a senior woman in my own organization at Wharton, I need to make that a priority and mentor younger women as well as men."

Lizann says that we may still be a generation away from a culture of gender-balanced leadership. There are men currently in leadership who won't change. The next generation is bringing more women and men who have been educated and trained and have worked in settings where the numbers of men and women were equal.

"That shared experience will prompt new models," Lizann says. "Quality of life is becoming a guiding issue for both men and women. It's now PC for men and women to want work-life integration. The fact is, women's traits make us change agents. I'm proud of being empathic: It helps build trust. Over time, the sociocultural messages have been strong: Men can't be warm, and women can't be aggressive. I have learned to navigate my professional culture in a way that I'm comfortable with and that maintains my integrity. If I have to curtail my aggressive tendencies, I'm smarter for doing so—and it's not necessarily because I'm a woman. It's because I want to be collaborative, respected and successful. It's not all or nothing. To be respected and treated equally we have to make some adjustments. We have to navigate successfully. It's just smart."

MARC CAMILLE

Marc Camille, PhD, is another vocal proponent of work-life balance. As vice president for enrollment management and communications of Loyola University Maryland, Marc is responsible for developing and managing Loyola's long-term enrollment and marketing strategies. Marc says that the best leaders lead by example. And he knows that to create balance, you need to communicate what that means. "You've got to be engaged, which requires active listening," Marc says. "Active listening is an essential leadership skill that, frankly speaking, most people lack. An engaged manager and an engaged colleague are more receptive to different perspectives, solutions or ideas. Women tend to be more adept at active listening, though not always. But women also seem to be able to develop the skill more easily and quickly than men."

We know that in most organizations fewer women are promoted to leadership roles. Marc says that that this lack of leadership opportunity has caused some women "to conclude they must be intensely competitive to advance."

Marc says there can be a better balance. "My advice to women— and men for that matter—is to focus first on delivering results by meeting job responsibilities and objectives. Develop a work philosophy so that you're effective, but not overly demanding or alienating. Don't forget what you experienced, and ultimately learned, along the way.

"When leadership opportunities are presented, be a difference maker, or a change agent. Keep things in perspective. It's one thing to advance your own career, and we all need opportunities to do so. And, in my opinion, it's equally important to pay it forward and back; foster a healthy, opportunistic and educational environment for younger women. Mentor those that follow you."

When we consider women's leadership opportunities and roles, we must also recognize the importance of work-life balance. "Family should not be sacrificed for work," Marc says. "Yes, there are times where the demands of work or opportunities for advancement will require family compromise or adaptation. But for those who have family obligations, recognize that's what it's about. A job and career should enhance rather than detract from your home life. In the case of women, or men, with young children, we all should be reminded that each day's events happen on that day only. Kids grow up quickly, and you can't get the time back. I don't think any burgeoning or established leader ever wants to be in a position where she or he looks back and says, I am so sorry to have missed that milestone in my child's life."

Of course, Marc understands that goals still need to be achieved and results delivered. "However, through creative thinking, a productive, successful work-life balance can be achieved," he says. "Job shares, staggered hours, or flex scheduling—whatever works."

Whether an employee works 8-5 or 10-7 is inconsequential if at the end of the day, the job is getting done and the organization's objectives are being advanced and achieved." —*Marc Camille*

10

THE FLEXIBLE WORKPLACE
Making Virtual Offices Work

In my mind, a flexible workplace is the way of the future. Let's embrace it. Realize it is not just about retaining talented women; Gen Y and the iGeneration, who will soon be 40% to 50% of our workforce, do their work well, often from Starbucks or from home, and often staying up till one or two a.m. If we don't offer flexibility, we will not attract or retain a large percentage of women and the two youngest generations. The virtual office is one way we will retain highly effective women and men who care about work-life balance.

Virtual employees meet with clients as needed and complete the majority of work from their home office. Working in a virtual office means fewer meetings and disruptions, and that leads to increased productivity and a greater level of contentment.

In this section, we hear from consultants who show how virtual work is good for business and share helpful tips to make this an effective option.

Celia de la Torre is CEO of Biztant, an office services company, which she manages from an office in her home. Celia believes that virtual offices are the forefront of the future. People who work in a virtual office are either telecommuters, working outside a corporate office, or entrepreneurs who are self-employed. Virtual offices are equipped with technology that enables business workers to restructure the support services of the traditional office. While this technology was either unavailable or much more expensive just a few years ago, it is now accessible and allows one to do business effectively and stay closely in touch from home.

"An exhilarating component of the virtual office," Celia shares, "is what it can do for people's personal lives. Traditional impediments of place and time no longer control the individual. The virtual office allows one to accomplish professional as well as personal goals."

Jeff Chapski agrees. Jeff's book *Career-ology: The Art and Science of a Successful Career,* is extremely helpful to college and graduate students positioning themselves to gain the career that will help them succeed and be happy. Jeff has important insights to share.

"Work-life balance is not just a women's issue," Jeff says. "Many men are stressed out today with business and family demands and they are not doing their best work. For those who are married or have partners, it's a family issue, and the couple needs to seek flexibility from their employers so they may do their best work professionally as well as have successful personal lives."

Marisa Peacock is CEO of the Strategic Peacock, a very successful online marketing firm. According to Marisa, "Working in a virtual environment can be tricky at first, but the benefits can be seen right away— no commuting, less time spent trying to book a conference room, fewer trips in your car to meet with clients, and more opportunities to work globally."

Here Marisa shares her ideas to help virtual teams work better and smarter together.

> **"Work-life balance is not just a women's issue. Many men are stressed out today with business and family demands and they are not doing their best work."**
> **—Jeff Chapski**

Her first tip is to designate office hours. "Let your clients and partners know when you'll be active online," she says. "They're welcome to ping, call or otherwise text you, but let them know that you may not be able to respond ASAP. Conveniently, virtual office hours don't need to be between 8-6. If you prefer to work earlier or later, let your constituents know. Even if you're online but unavailable to talk, be sure to set your status to busy."

Marisa also recommends using collaborative platforms. "Simplify your work life," she says. "Explore social business platforms that encourage better collaboration. Networks like Yammer or Mavenlink can become a hub for clients that allow for private discussions, document sharing and project management. Many of these sites allow for mobile access, so you can stay up-to-date with client communications while on the go."

She also says that sometimes you just need to get outside. "Your home office may be your home base, but it's important to enjoy the benefits of working virtually," she says. "When you can, explore working from different locations and don't be hesitant to take calls while on the go. A virtual office affords the luxury of experimenting, finding what are the best ways for you to get your work done well and to enjoy yourself. There's no need to be glued to your desk."

Amanda Doyle is a policy analyst with Education First Consulting, a firm with no offices, not a one. Everyone in the company works virtually. A graduate of the University of Virginia and Georgetown's School of Public Policy, Amanda was editor-in-chief of the *Georgetown Public Policy Review*, an important publication in the public policy world.

Working at home for Amanda means working from her living room, on the same schedule and deadlines as her virtual colleagues. She has some insights to share from this experience.

"Like most working environments, having a home office makes some things easier and some things harder. Working from home provides a lot of benefits. There are the obvious benefits: you don't have to commute, you don't have to invest in a professional wardrobe, you can take a power nap to refresh instead of chugging coffee, you can go to the gym in the middle of the day, you can drop off and pick up your kids from school, you can hang out with your cat all day, and so on.

"As a young professional, however, I've noticed some less obvious perks. For instance, work is about work. I get a lot done. I read without distraction. I don't have to try and block out conversations happening in the next cubicle. As a consequence, I learn a lot. I research and analyze just like I did in grad school, only now I get paid for it! Another perk specific to me is that my clients (often state education leaders) don't know that I'm young. Sure, they could go on the website and read my bio, but more often than not I get to be judged based on my intellect, either my writing or my ability to facilitate conversations over the phone. As a particularly young looking twenty-eight-year-old, this is cool. I don't have to wear heels to look more professional or glasses to look smarter. I just do what I do and let my work stand for itself."

Despite these perks, Amanda still sees some downsides to working virtually. "Obviously, the flip side of being a young professional working from home is that I miss out on a lot of social interaction," she says. "I miss coffee breaks with coworkers or gossiping at the water cooler. Though I attend organized happy hours, I don't ever spontaneously pop out for a drink after a hard day with a group of my peers. I like to think, though, that compared to the intellect I'm gaining, these are small sacrifices.

"The major negative is that thought partnership is harder. I can't just walk into someone's office and ask for a quick opinion. Don't get me wrong, I have check-ins all the time, and many, many times I just pick up the phone and see if I can catch someone to share an idea. However, it's just not the same as walking down the hall. On the one hand, my problem-solving skills are getting really strong. On the other hand, the firm is missing out on a lot of great ideas because we can't as readily bounce thoughts off of one another. We just started professional learning communities, though, and I'm hoping these will be transformative."

Amanda's next insight is about culture. "A firm that chooses to have a virtual working environment does not necessarily place less emphasis on building strong organizational culture than more traditional work environments," she says. "Though we don't have a central office, my firm is obsessed with creating a strong organizational culture. They have achieved this goal better than any other organization for which I've worked. We have a buddy system, a mentor system, monthly calls, biannual retreats, a 360 review process, regular emphasis on how to improve feedback, organized happy hours and dinners, and the list goes on and on. When I expressed some trouble adjusting to the virtual environment I was smothered with options. 'Should we rent some office space for you? How can we help?' We have a human capital committee that focuses on these issues, and they do a wonderful job."

Amanda also finds that bigger-picture motivation is a good culture builder. "My firm's theory of action is not that having people work virtually will save them money, though that was likely a driving factor when they set up shop seven years ago. Instead, it's that the best people are spread out across the country, and if they let people work where they already live, they can attract the best talent."

> **"Deadlines are deadlines, clients are clients, analyzing policy is difficult. Nothing about remote work feels different to me."**
> **—Amanda Doyle**

For her last insight, Amanda wants to debunk a myth: "Working from home is often not 'more relaxing' than working in an office."

She says her day is very busy. "I'm on calls almost all day long," she says. "Working from home doesn't mean that I can slack off. I may be wearing yoga pants, but being unprepared for a meeting is being unprepared for a meeting! A firm with a virtual working environment can still be highly intense and stressful. Deadlines are deadlines, clients are clients, analyzing policy is difficult. Nothing about remote work feels different to me."

TAYLOR SCHICHE AND KATIE BARONGAN

I do leadership coaching with Billy Casper Golf in northern Virginia, the leading golf course management company in the United States. They manage more than 150 courses throughout the country and employ about seven thousand people. In our conversations, I have often heard people refer to Taylor Schiche, a dynamite HR professional who worked remotely for them for over three years. Taylor has moved on to an opportunity with a company close to her home to accommodate her young family.

Previously, while Taylor was with Billy Casper Golf, people around the company said over and over again how helpful she was. Seldom did someone mention that she was in North Dakota, completely off site almost all of the time. I had to talk with her, get her ideas for this book. How did she accomplish this seamless HR presence, working remotely?

Taylor is a mother with more than ten years of talent management experience with various industries, handling recruitment, performance management and compensation. She knew that to be effective as a telecommuting HR professional and as a mother, she had to juggle many responsibilities. The first thing she recommends is, "It is essential to have good child support. A mom has to be comfortable or it will be a real strain." Taylor says she definitely valued the flexibility of working from home. If one of her children was ill, she was right there.

How did she get the opportunity to telecommute? "When my husband was to be transferred to Bismarck, my boss asked me if I would like to work part time, telecommuting from there until she found my replacement. Well, fortunately, she liked my work. She said it was just what was needed, and she offered me a full-time role.

"At Billy Casper Golf, I realized how important it was to be in regular communication with everyone I needed to work with," Taylor says. "I know how important the clarity of my communication is, and I always tried to think about that. To me, the key is to pick up the phone. I do use email, but I am also a believer in verbal conversations so that nothing is lost. When I receive a request for help, and I receive lots of them, I try to call immediately, or if I'm in the middle of something and cannot do what's being asked right away, I still call to ask if I may get back to them as soon I am finished."

People appreciate responsiveness. Taylor was promoted to a larger role with regional HR responsibilities. She worked on company-wide initiatives such as employee relations, performance management and career portals. Taylor was always included in weekly HR team meetings and stayed current on activities throughout the company. She did some travel as needed, such as attending annual and regional meetings.

She says she has learned a lot from working virtually. "What I have learned is that attitude is very important," she says. "If we want to do a great job, we can. It's been easy for me to have a positive attitude. I love what I do and appreciate any opportunity to work from my home."

However, she admits that attitude isn't everything. "It's also important to keep up with the state of the art of your field," she says. "I am active with my SHRM (Society of Human Resource Management) network. In fact, I am president elect of our local chapter."

She says she has also learned the importance of prioritization, "to use my judgment, to look at my emails and listen to my phone messages and decide which are the top priorities."

Taylor successfully worked remotely for three years. She then decided she wanted more face time, more regular interaction with management on site. She wanted to travel more, but the timing wasn't right. Her husband was then called on to travel more for his job. And her kids were still young. Reluctantly, Taylor decided to leave the company.

> **"It's been easy for me to have a positive attitude. I love what I do and appreciate any opportunity to work from my home."**
> **—Taylor Schiche**

With Taylor's permission, we spoke with her boss, Katie Barongan, V.P. Human Resources, so we could learn more about this arrangement and pass on lessons in this book.

"Taylor always had a lot of great ideas," Katie says. "I always told people, 'the reason we're doing this is because of Taylor.' I always sent her handwritten cards to thank her. She wasn't in the office to stand up and be recognized in front of her peers, so I thought maybe a card on the fridge would be good, that she could feel good in front of her family."

I asked Katie what she would do differently, in hindsight, to try to keep Taylor at the company. Katie says, "We tried everything to keep her, but the reality is Taylor was highly recruited by a locally based company that was very high tech and with her husband's new responsibilities and his travel demands, it just made sense for Taylor to accept the job opportunity so she could be close to home as needed with her babies."

Taylor loved the people of Billy Casper Golf, their trust in her and in her work, but this is her time to be with her young children. She does say she might come back to Billy Casper Golf in the future as her family responsibilities change. Taylor recognizes that Katie Barongan in HR, Alex Elmore, chief operating officer, and other company leaders are very people and family oriented. Together, they work to accommodate the needs of their people.

PART V

DRIVING CHANGE

FORTUNATELY, AN INCREASING NUMBER of companies are developing excellent strategies for change. In this chapter, we learn how to effect culture changes that will strengthen leadership and improve results. Lisa Loehr, an extremely talented HR professional, details a change in management protocol that will retain and incorporate high-potential women.

We also learn here from Emily Holland White, an insightful HR professional who has done important research on the specific issues facing mothers returning to work—and how we can retain them. We now know that if we want our companies to succeed, we need women in senior leadership so they may positively impact our culture, our spirit and our financial results. Of course, to do that, we must be willing to accommodate the need for flexibility in the workplace, especially for women who have childcare and eldercare responsibilities. What matters are results, not hours at a desk.

In the next chapter, we will learn how our team members can stay connected with clients, colleagues and work while raising children, caring for elderly parents or simply having a balanced life!

We must remember that true leadership comes from our attitude. There is no "off the shelf" way to share leadership within your company. If you want to be a forward-thinking leader and bring highly capable women onto your leadership team, there are a great many things to consider. Certainly, senior management must be fully and genuinely supportive. It must be an imperative.

Once you have senior management on board, believing that leadership can be improved, then I urge that women and men in your company have input on how to make it happen within your company, particularly with regard to flexibility.

Some of the flexible work environments in place today are not really achieving their goals. They are not widely accepted, often because the line managers do not believe the value.

Studies show that companies that actively implement and support coaching and mentoring programs are more profitable.

We must empower high potential women to self-advocate for leadership positions. How do we do that? Institute durable coaching and mentoring programs that support women throughout their career. This is critical to developing leadership skills and confidence. Studies show that companies that actively implement and support coaching and mentoring programs are more profitable.[37] Why? Because they are much more likely to attract and retain strong talent!

Yet beyond coaching and networking, women must develop financial and business proficiencies. It is essential to know the business you're in. What makes it work? What is needed to help it grow? Growing the business, especially generating new clients, is an excellent way for women to position themselves for promotion. Show your boss how you are adding value, and you will definitely be noticed! We especially need to support women in the financial services, where there are very few women in leadership, and where their risk awareness is sorely needed. Honestly, all women aspiring and growing into more challenging roles can benefit from ongoing support and guidance.

Will a mentor or coaching program guarantee career longevity? Maybe not, but it will certainly help retain the best talent, and help to empower women to advocate for promotions and for work-life balance, both of which will lead to long-term career satisfaction and success, for all of us!

Remember, it is up to leadership to make the changes that will enable talented women to thrive in the workforce.

LISA LOEHR

Lisa Loehr is the founder and president of Loehr Consulting, an HR coaching business partnering with small and midsize businesses. Lisa has a Total HR Performance Portfolio—broad and deep experience in primary HR functions in high technology, software development, manufacturing, nonprofit, healthcare and customer service firms. Prior to developing her own HR firm, Lisa was VP of operations at the Wilderness Society and before that director of HR at Samsung Semiconductor.

> **"If you can't measure it, you can't manage it."**
> **—W. Edwards Deming**

> **"If you can't measure it, you can't improve it."**
> **—Peter Drucker**

Here, Lisa advises us on issues to consider when designing flextime, and she details the procedure for an effective CMP, change management plan.

I suggest we all study ROWE—Results-Only Work Environment—prior to implementing a CMP. Studies have shown that offering increased autonomy via work flex retains workers because employees feel they have more professional choices to impact their current situation —they stay and change from within rather than acting on the natural impulse to leave. At the same time, creating autonomy allows employees the flexibility they need to manage their personal life.

While it is important to invest time and develop policy solutions to attract and retain high-performing women, I suggest your organization consider a shift to motivation-based solutions that are gender neutral. By serving the entire workforce, you promote greater retention and improved performance while inherently addressing work-life issues that impact all staff.

LET'S GO THROUGH THE PROCESS
OF A CHANGE MANAGEMENT PLAN.
These are the key elements:

Culture – Driven by leadership, the culture of the organization is a cluster of values, behaviors and expectations—some spoken and others unspoken. The more better defined a culture is, the more helpful in terms of creating a successful loop from hiring to retention. Clarity from the onset allows staff members, and especially women, to self-select the organizations that are most aligned with both their personal values and individual/family needs.

Communication – As with all work environments, getting beyond the facts and figures of the company's performance is critical to an inclusive work environment. We need to demonstrate to our team members, ideally all of them, that we value and trust them by sharing as much appropriate information as we can. How do the senior managers work with their people, are there conversations or do they rely heavily on email and newsletters? How receptive are senior managers to ideas from the people doing the work of the company? Do people feel trusted as information is readily shared, or is it more on a need-to-know basis? Do senior managers ask for ideas, advice and feedback? Do they listen to understand and learn? This is how we connect and fully engage our people.

Technology – this creates more buy-in. While Generation Y is firmly rooted in the workplace, Generation Z (fondly known as the iGeneration, or Internet Generation) is just entering the workforce. This group has not known life without the World Wide Web and is comfortable on multiple devices—not just a home or work computer— and tends to communicate more through IM'ing, texting or video such as Skype or Facetime via iPhone.

By making the investment in mobile devices and policies that enable staff to accomplish work via technology, organizations have the potential to achieve the ultimate in building an autonomous workforce.

TASKS FOR THE EXECUTIVE TEAM:

A. **First develop a baseline and momentum. This will be a culture change—successful change requires a call to action along with a CMP (change management plan) and feedback mechanism.**

   1. CMP general outline

- Conduct series of exercises across corporation showing power of diversity (using common exercises and HBR case studies)

- Convey a call of action by CEO (Why, Where, How, When, WIIFM)

2. Develop CMP

- State call to action

- Present current state assessment

- Define goal state

- Define implementation

B. METRICS on diversity are a must (goals and actuals)

1. Utilize diversity coaching using common methods to show how a diverse management team ALWAYS outperforms a nondiverse team

2. Brown bags with senior execs and outside senior female execs as an education tool

3. Early hiring of a senior renowned female exec to demonstrate commitment

4. Part of CMP training at all levels: Words and deeds matter. Become aware of gender-biased language, including inappropriate jokes. Zero tolerance policy on sexual harassment

TASKS FOR MANAGERS:

A. Potentially the single most important relationship at work is between a woman and her manager. If this is not strong, a woman should be prepared to leave and find a manager who will help her succeed.

B. There are significant ways managers must support women at work:

1. Providing regular feedback

2. Delivering growth-oriented performance reviews

3. Mentorship, training/education

4. Promotion

5. Compensation

6. Flexible work options

C. **Respect/professionalism**

1. All staff takes cues from individuals in leadership roles, and this indicates to them how they are to treat others.

2. "Titanium Rule" (treat others the way THEY want to be treated).

D. **Offer a wide network to assist staffers in gaining knowledge and enjoying success on the job.**

E. **Serve as a reference moving laterally or upward within an organization—or when moving on to next opportunity.**

TASKS FOR PEERS:

A. **Women can help themselves by taking responsibility for developing strong peer relationships.**

B. **Women need to seek coaching advice.**

1. To work on increasing inner confidence and to value your skills, to present your true self at the table by sharing your ideas and asking important questions, and certainly to gain the respect, opportunities and rewards you deserve. Realize that it is important to say what you think. And it's okay not to agree, especially if you express yourself with respect. It is also and especially important to build your inner confidence.

2. A woman should learn what aspect of her ability to form strong internal relationships at all levels is challenging—whether it is having difficulty making idle conversation or conflict of per-

sonal needs over work priorities that interfere with informal opportunities.

a. Create a plan to meet the challenge.

TASKS FOR HUMAN RESOURCES:

A. Provide support to the executive team and management by facilitating an inclusive work environment.

B. Via the CMP, HR supports the evolving workplace needs and collaboratively reviews the following for alignment with culture:

1. Handbook/policies and procedures

2. Pay practices/actual compensation

3. Performance management systems/outcomes (review ratings)

4. Promotions

5. Education/Training

    a. Benefits—including "gender/family sensitive" such as: flex work, support for working families (dependent care), elder care, and support for singles

    b. Succession planning

Finally, be aware, the new trend is that more people are living alone. Nearly 30% of the adult population now live by themselves, and the number is growing. This creates a new stress at work—think of all the people juggling a home along with, potentially, the needs of a child/children, elderly parents, pets, health issues—and not having support from a life partner. Companies that acknowledge this and provide assistance via services will be ahead of the game. Examples of services that help single people are: concierge, on-site dry-cleaning pickup, flex work, pet insurance, reimbursement for some personal expenses while on travel, elder care insurance.

> **"My advice is to partner with your HR executive and create a checklist to ensure that all of the tasks, while seemingly obvious, are optimized."**
> **—Lisa Loehr**

As an HR professional, I've seen small and large businesses do some or most of the tasks I've outlined in this chapter well, but rarely all of them. My advice is to partner with your HR executive and create a checklist to ensure that all of the tasks, while seemingly obvious, are optimized.

A crucial part of the discussion about work-life balance is addressing the issues that women face when returning to work following maternity leave or family care leave. Emily Holland White is a recent graduate of the Strategic Human Capital Management program at Georgetown University. She is a Senior Director of Talent & Culture at Optoro. Emily's research, in the section below, shows us how organizations can help talented women reenter the work place following maternity and other leaves.

EMILY HOLLAND WHITE

Despite well-established legislation aimed at promoting gender equality, such as Title IX, the Family and Medical Leave Act and the Civil Rights Act, the gender gap in business leadership has stalled. One of the main reasons for this persistent gender gap is related to the career interruptions and exits that professional women partake in after becoming new mothers.

Beginning in the 1980s, scholars identified a trend of high-achieving women "returning home," as they redirected priorities towards their families and not their careers. The media reinforced this trend by frequently reporting whenever a high-powered woman left her career and cited as her sole reason the need to become a full-time mother.

Three companies, Ernst & Young, Goldman Sachs and Lehman Brothers, sponsored a survey to investigate the role of off-ramps and on-ramps in the career trajectories of 2,443 highly qualified and professional women.[38] The study ultimately found that the opt-out trend is attributed to "pull factors" (family obligations at home) and "push factors" (features of the employer or job that make it difficult for mothers to balance both sets of responsibilities).

The decision to take a career interruption or exit was found to be difficult and drawn out for most women in the study, as they felt they had invested much time and energy in their careers and did not want to leave it all behind. Despite appearing traditional in their decision to return to a gender role at home, these women were contemporary in their desires to combine work and family, and felt both a severe loss of identity after making the decision to leave their careers and pain about their inability to do both.

In fact, many women who opt out are surprised that they are stay-at-home moms, as they had aspired to combine both family and career —but the rigidity of their workplaces made it impossible to balance both work and family. The literature recommends that managers explore the true reasons why mothers decide to off-ramp so they can better address the workplace issues causing them to leave.

> **"The overwhelming majority of mothers intend to return to the workforce after taking a career interruption (93%), but they usually do not understand the challenges they will face when they do return."**
> **—Emily Holland White**

Current research by Pamela Stone found that 90% of women cited workplace problems as the deciding "push" factor to leave—more specifically, the long and demanding hours. Rigid leave policies made working mothers feel the push factors more, resulting in a perception that they needed to make an "all or nothing decision."[39] The overwhelming majority of mothers intend to return to the workforce after taking a career interruption (93%), but they usually do not understand the challenges they will face when they do return. Research has found mothers want to return to work for a multitude of reasons, including financial independence as well as the satisfaction they receive from their careers. In addition, Hewlett and Luce's groundbreaking study uncovered a new and surprising reason why working mothers want to return: a desire to give something back to the community through purpose-driven work.[40]

The time mothers spend at home away from their careers often results in changed aspirations, specifically a desire to work with people they respect, to be themselves, to have flexibility and to give back to the community. The Kaleidoscope Career Model describes how both men's and women's career patterns shift over time as their

needs and interests change. Women prioritize challenge in the begin-
ning of their career, balance in mid-career and authenticity later in
their career.

This new focus on purpose-driven work may also explain why so
few women (5%) return to their employers when they do pursue on-
ramping back into their careers. Their changing motivations, desires
and needs related to career may not fit well into the demands and
culture of their original career paths and employers.

Often, women feel that the off-ramped time away from work seri-
ously impacts their linear career trajectory, and thus their ability to
advance and develop as working professionals. This perceived depre-
cation of their skill set and increased interest in meeting the needs of
their children leads to mothers giving up their careers and starting
over. This shift and change in career direction impacts their economic
and social power, as many careers in female-dominated industries are
low paid and low status. However, professions such as teaching or
nursing offer flexibility and reduced-hour options.

The substantial shift that working mothers experience related to
their career orientations and preferences has implications for em-
ployers and the workforce in general, as these women who are willing
to give up their careers and start over in a different industry or pro-
fession lose their skill set and talent, from the original employers'
perspective.

Penalties of time out of the workforce are in fact severe. While the
average time women off-ramp is only 2.2 years, these short interrup-
tions of work result in stark financial penalties and loss of potential
opportunities. Research shows that on average women lose 18% of
their earning power when they off-ramp, and lose on average 28% of
their earning power if they work in the financial services industry. For
those women who opt to off-ramp for a longer time period, two to three
years, they can lose on average 38% of their earning power.[41] *This loss*
of earning power makes on-ramping back into the workforce less ap-
pealing and oftentimes does not make financial sense, given the high
cost of childcare.

The best outcome of this research would be that organizations ac-
cept the fact that working mothers will take time off from work due to

family obligations, and develop strategies to maintain connections with the mothers during this off-ramp time period. Hewlett and Luce recommend creating reduced hours jobs that include flexibility in the day and also in the arch of careers, but warned that these efforts will only be successful if the stigma and discrimination associated with such work arrangements are removed. They highlight the importance of organizational culture and its impact on the success of policies and procedures aimed to support working mothers. Their research suggests that "the transformation of the corporate culture seems to be a prerequisite for success on the work-life front," and they urge organizations to understand the complexities of women's nonlinear careers and unique needs and to develop strategies to support rather than discriminate those who off-ramp and on-ramp back into the workforce.

We know that working mothers often leave jobs because of the stigma associated with flexible options. Many women attempt to continue their career paths by seeking out part-time or reduced hours, but find that these perceived solutions actually became the real problem. One-third of the women report "hours creep," part-time arrangements that were in fact full time, but without the full-time pay and benefits.

In fact, the working mothers' flexible work arrangements resulted in less enjoyable and stimulating work, with the more strategic responsibilities being eliminated, and their skills not fully utilized. These women also feel that despite their efforts to remain in the workforce, they were seen as second-class citizens due to their flexible work arrangements.

While many organizations are falling short to meet the needs of working mothers, many others are trying in earnest to do so but fail to implement the desired strategies effectively. The failure of these efforts may be attributable to three factors: (1) flexible work options granted at the discretion of managers, rather than a uniform, company-wide policy; (2) the extent to which the flexible work options are only associated with working mothers rather than all employees; and (3) the way in which the flexible options are offered as a private favor and pitched as a secret reward.

Therefore, the fact that flexible work options are not fully rooted into the organization's culture results in their fragile and unsuccessful nature.

Working mothers and employers can create a win-win solution by creating policies that promote career continuity, not interruption, and encourage women to opt in by making it possible to balance both family and work in a meaningful and stigma-free manner. In order for these policies to be successful, they must be deeply rooted in the corporate culture, so the norms that govern the workplace support flexible work arrangements and nonlinear career paths that working mothers need to take.

Employers need to redefine what it means to be a productive and committed employee, and acknowledge that all employees have obligations outside work, not just working mothers.

11

LEADERS AT THE FOREFRONT

Certainly, many companies want to be a great place for women to work and enjoy success in both their business and their personal lives. It's not easy, because women have so much in the way of responsibilities, and they have needs that change over time and are not always predictable.

Attitude is everything. If the most senior people in a company are committed to finding ways for their talented women to combine their business careers and their personal responsibilities, they are most likely to be successful.

What I've learned in my work and in conversations with the leaders profiled here is that often the CEO and human resource, organizational development and talent development professionals understand the importance of promoting women, but the people out in the field do not share that same commitment and passion, and they do not accept the importance of the company's commitment to be women and family friendly. Therefore, the effort to offer balance gets watered down.

We need women's skills *now*— and today's technology allows us to work virtually and still be highly productive and give excellent client service.

I've been told that at times, someone's boss—often a man—will say, "We have flex time available," in such a way that women know right away that he does not encourage them to take advantage of it. This is because the existing culture doesn't support it. I have heard many stories from women who have become discouraged about the lack of opportunities to work remotely, even for a period of time.

This is not the way to a bright future. We need women's business and leadership skills now—and today's technology allows us to work virtually and still be highly productive and give excellent client service. The world uses Skype, Lynk, instant messaging, the phone and email, as well as face-to-face meetings when important.

People in business, at all levels in their companies, need to understand that helping women to continue their career trajectories is good for everyone. This will improve financial results. It's the smart thing to do. This has to be communicated and supported a lot better than it has been in most companies.

In this section, we profile exemplary leaders who understand the value that talented women are bringing to their companies. Len Gemma, COO of Lockton DC, understands this: he has worked alongside women in business who were absolute stars in their expertise and commitment to clients, and he saw the positive impact they had on company growth and organizational culture. So now, in his leadership position at Lockton, Len seeks to recruit highly talented women and provide professional development programs as well as opportunities for women to work effectively while caring for their children and their other family responsibilities.

We also profile Tom Bozzuto and Julie Smith, chairman and president, respectively, of The Bozzuto Group, a very successful and well-run commercial property company in the D.C. area. Tom and Julie have a great partnership. They each know what the other is good at, and they work together with the greatest of respect—clearly wanting to provide the people in the company with the benefits of their combined leadership competencies.

We will also hear from another great partnership, Neil Shah and Lily Cua, who were classmates in the McDonough School of Business at Georgetown. They learned about entrepreneurial principles together and decided to match up their very different skill sets and start up Aspire, a software company that allows every employee of a company to customize her or his employee benefits. This is timely, of course, as we know job appreciation and satisfaction drive retention and results. Neil has endless ideas, and Lily is pragmatic and analytical. As classmates and now as business partners on a dynamic venture, gender has no place in their thought process.

The final leader we profile in this book is Arthur Woods, a social entrepreneur working in operations, design and positive psychology, and founder of his company, Imperative. Arthur tells us how women are shaping the future of the workplace.

Let's be part of the evolving business world, and let's expedite change! Let's listen and learn from the forward-thinking leadership of Len Gemma, Tom Bozzuto, Julie Smith, Neil Shah and Lily Cua, and Arthur Woods.

Companies with forward-thinking leaders are thriving with gender-diverse leadership. They are true leaders of this exciting movement to advance women to senior leadership.

LEN GEMMA

Len Gemma and the Lockton Companies are innovators at the forefront of the movement to increase the share of women in leadership. Len is chief operating officer of Lockton's operations in Washington, D.C. He previously was a managing director of Marsh and president of Johnson & Higgins in Baltimore. Len has worked in the insurance brokerage industry for thirty years, a world dominated by male leaders overseeing large teams, often heavily populated by women in more junior roles.

In his many years working with different types of leaders with different levels of skill, Len says he has learned that promoting women to leadership is essential to success. "Companies that are prospering are comprised of people with different skills and common goals," he says. "Not taking advantage of the leadership skills of 50% of the population in your business is not going to maximize your outcome for your clients, owners or colleagues. The number of women in business leadership hasn't changed much during the past forty years. That seems shortsighted to me."

Len says that diverse leadership isn't about generalizing about gender roles. It is about embracing each individual's gifts. "An enlightened workplace embraces gender and other differences as an opportunity to create a truly high performing organization," he says.

"Businesses run more smoothly with people who have complementary skill sets. We know that women often bring a sense of community and compassion to the workplace. This can be a game changer, converting a quiet, isolative work environment to an energetic, interactive and collaborative culture. Men have less of a need to like each other to work together. They'll just ignore someone they don't like and say, 'Just throw me the ball and let's get the job done.' Women I've worked with are guided by a sense of fairness and standards of behavior that are required in order to be part of a team. These women are more collegial, and their teams often function at a higher level."

This skill and the importance women place on connection are important to the future workplace, according to Len. "Women seem to want to feel connected to coworkers and other women, but don't see structure in terms of a hierarchy as much as a web," he says. "As businesses become flatter and collaboration is more important than compliance, these are the skill sets that are increasingly important for an effective workplace."

At Lockton, the prospective employee interview process involves a series of meetings with a cross section of associates followed by a feedback session where all of the interviewers discuss pros and cons of each candidate. "While both men and women are attuned to cultural fit," Len says, "women often see the potential coworker as much as an addition to the community as they do someone who brings technical expertise to the business."

There have been several great examples of women developing talent management and talent acquisition programs within Lockton's D.C.-based business. Each relates to strengthening the community and therefore the business as a whole. One such effort involves how Lockton uses its internship program as a means of identifying candidates who will be a good long-term fit for business. Another involves the onboarding procedure for new associates. "Both are critical, people-oriented endeavors that help us compete more effectively in the war for talent," Len says. "Both were conceived and led by very talented women in our business: the first by Sheila Johnson with our internship program, the next by Cait Crivella with onboarding."

Lockton's Washington, D.C. office used personal networks to

recruit top talent from local competitors from the beginning. "While the strategy proved successful in the first few years, it presented challenges in the long run," Len says. "It became increasingly costly to continue hiring tenured employees, competitor talent was limited, and our business was not developing a pipeline of entry-level people to groom, support and grow with the organization long term. As a result, leadership deemed recruiting through an internship program a top company priority."

Once the idea was accepted, the program had to be developed. "We shared the plan with associates in a company-wide meeting," Len says. "I volunteered to spearhead the internship program along-side a member of the leadership team, Jason Jones. I worked with a team to develop a targeted recruiting strategy that started at George-town University. We established a formal interview process that in-volved several members of the department. The comprehensive re-cruiting process was critical, as it ensured that the candidate fit in with the culture and that colleagues had buy-in on our selections.

"We then designed a twelve-week development program, which included client projects, weekly trainings, a trip to our headquarters in Kansas City to meet with top leadership, and a final case study to be presented to local leaders in D.C."

The curriculum gave the leaders insight into the interns' capabili-ties and aptitude for learning, while determining whether they fit in with the Lockton culture. As a result, it was easy for Lockton to iden-tify whom they wanted to extend an offer to at the end of the pro-gram. After the first year, they extended offers to two interns, who joined them full time last summer. The program has since been em-ulated across departments. Lockton has expanded its list of targeted schools for recruitment and continues to grow from the bottom up.

The feedback has been positive from leaders and interns alike. Len shares a note that one intern wrote the feedback form. "Some-thing I have taken away from this internship that I was not expecting to learn is that one of the most important things about where you work is the people you work with and the kind of environment you work in."

Lockton D.C. has grown exponentially in revenue and head count

The goals of Lockton's Women in Leadership program are to maximize business opportunities for Lockton women and enhance leadership skills through networking and more formalized professional development and mentorship.

since the office opened in 2005. Conversations in the mentorship program affirm that there is great pride in what has been built, and associates are clearly committed to the success of the company and to each other. Len says. "In this culture, it is natural that individuals are rising to the occasion to assist new hires and make them feel part of Lockton. Our key leaders stayed involved and always available to mentor."

Beyond these specific examples of building dynamic, collaborative culture, Lockton has developed WIL, a women in leadership program headed by Claudia Mandato, an EVP based in the Kansas City headquarters, and Lisa Wall, a risk finance executive. The goals of Lockton's women in leadership program are to maximize business opportunities for Lockton women and enhance leadership skills through networking and more formalized professional development and mentorship.

These initiatives demonstrate that by developing a strong team and tapping into complementary skill sets, a truly high-performing culture can be created and nurtured.

TOM BOZZUTO AND JULIE SMITH

To demonstrate a terrific example of successful shared leadership, Adrienne and I interviewed Tom Bozzuto and Julie Smith, co-leaders at The Bozzuto Group real estate company. Their spirit of enterprise combined with their progressive attitudes and flexible work policies make them an ideal partnership for study.

During his forty-year career, Tom Bozzuto has overseen the creation of nearly fifty thousand residential units valued at nearly $7 billon. In 1988, Tom was a founder of The Bozzuto Group. Today, the company provides a broad range of real estate services, including development, management, homebuilding, acquisitions and construction. In his role as CEO, Tom directs the development, con-

struction and management of income-producing and for-sale hous-
ing in metropolitan areas located throughout the East Coast.

As president of Bozzuto Management Company, Julie Smith oversees a portfolio that includes nearly forty thousand units in more
than 150 apartment communities throughout the Mid-Atlantic and
Northeastern regions. She is also a consultant in the development of
new communities both for Bozzuto and third-party owners, providing marketing and management guidance in the planning stages of
new projects. Under Julie's leadership, the company has grown from
an organization with fifteen employees to one of more than eight
hundred, and has twice been named Property Management Firm of
the Year by the National Association of Home Builders (NAHB). Julie
Smith was named *Multifamily Executive Magazine*'s 2013 Executive
of the Year.

Tom and Julie were interviewed together for this book. It is their
partnership and openness that make them strong leaders. First, they
shared their view on women's leadership.

"If you exclude women, you're excluding 50% of the population,"
Tom says. "Having said that, I believe that talent doesn't discriminate by gender or nationality. And
you're a damn fool if you don't look
for talent any place you can find it.
There are certainly as many brilliant women as there are brilliant
men. I don't think you can general-
ize about women and men's business skills."

> **"I believe that talent doesn't discriminate by gender or nationality. And you're a damn fool if you don't look for talent any place you can find it."**
> **—Tom Bozzuto**

Julie believes that discriminative
hiring or promotion practices are not the whole reason there are
fewer women in leadership. "The issue with too few women in leadership is a logistical problem, more than anything else," she says.
"There is a twelve- to fifteen-year challenging period when women
and men are raising families. That is one of the reasons more women
aren't at the top. You've got to get through that period of time, which
is often the most critical ladder-climbing period of career advancement in many professions. What are required for women's advance-

ment are family-friendly policies, flexibility and an open mindset. There are women in their forties and fifties who can be helpful to younger women by sharing their experience, yet many women who have been there can be tough on younger women, thinking, 'I did it, so can you.'"

She says that technology is one possible solution. "You don't want to lose productivity during those tough years," she says. "Virtual work is the direction the industry is heading, and it will make a difference for many women who are juggling both family and careers."

It is up to leadership to make the changes that will enable women to stay in the workforce. Julie says, "They need to put flexibility on the agenda. Our company oversees forty thousand apartments in 150 locations along the East Coast. We've got to have ten-hour coverage in our field offices, so we can offer four ten-hour day workweeks and provide full-time employment with all benefits included. This is a huge win-win. The business is fully covered, and it allows employees one more day at home. Our accounting group can provide two shifts a day; 7 a.m. to 3 p.m. day, or 3 p.m. to 11 p.m. and provide even more flexibility. It's just a matter of doing it. You've got to commit to being creative. It takes time and effort to think openly about this. And you must be realistic about challenges. For example, in this area, we try to help people avoid the long driving commutes during rush hour traffic because it ultimately costs both the employee and the business. So flexible schedules in this regard can benefit both the business and the employee."

Tom agrees that flexibility is the way of the future. "The younger generation seems to be going back to wanting to work from home, to be with the kids," he says. "There are a couple of variables here. People need to change, and the workplace needs to change to make this work. What is happening now with virtual work will allow more women to maintain their positions. Corporations that are changing their work standards are recognizing that there's a tremendous pool of talent in women."

For Tom this is a talent acquisition problem as well as a talent retention problem. "Look at college graduation rates over the past ten years," he says. "There has been a dramatic increase in women graduates. If I want to be sure that I continue to get the high caliber of people, the top talent I expect in my organization, I have to be flexible toward women."

Julie says that to remain competitive "organizations need to be culturally aware, innovative, and sensitive to address the needs of all employees at all stages of their lives. Real estate leadership has always been male dominated. That will change slowly. But in the meantime, we need to have office managers who know that some women returning from maternity leave will need a lactation room, for example, among other kinds of support."

Tom agrees that support is necessary, and if women want to progress to leadership this support is going to have to happen at home as well as in the office. "Well, you can't take yourself out for twelve years and come back in at the same level," he says. "What has changed, though, and will continue to change, is that more men are comfortable in positions where they are working from home. I'm on the board of an art museum in Baltimore, and we just hired an extraordinary executive director. Her husband is a freelance curator who works from home while caring for their nine-year-old twins. He made the decision that he will lead an independent career life as a consultant, and it is working well for their family. He is the anchor at home. And, as I have always said to Julie, you've got to have someone like Richard, her husband, who holds down the fort at home."

> "When I was in the thick of things, when my babies were small, Tom said to me, 'I'm not going tell you how to do this, but I know you'll figure it out.' What I have learned is that everyone needs to be willing to compromise, and it's not going to be perfect."
> —Julie Smith

Julie agrees. "We have a culture of support," she says. "Family is first, but everyone knows that the work has to get done, too. When I was in the thick of things, when my babies were small, Tom said to me, 'I'm not going tell you how to do this, but I know you'll figure it out.' What I have learned is that everyone needs to be willing to compromise, and it's not going to be perfect. I learned that the hard way. Women have to be more realistic about what has to give along the way in order for the work to get done while you are juggling family responsibilities. What I tell women with young children or sick family members is that you'll never work harder than you do right now. These are the toughest years. And it's ok to say, 'I'm so tired.' That openness is important. It puts everyone on an even playing field."

Tom says that they try to think of employees' well-being as much as possible. "One of the reasons we have our office where we do is because we know women will have to leave at a moment's notice to pick up a child who's sick at school," he says. "We have never had a time clock. We have a man in leadership whose teenager has a serious illness. When he has to go, he goes."

"The bottom line, as Julie has emphasized, is that leadership has to be empathic to be successful," Tom says. "We all know the guy who's a jock and talks only to guys. I couldn't work in that environment. Our company has always tried to be open, honest and willing to listen. We're all in this together, and will only make it work if we pull together."

Working together with respect and honesty is what makes Tom and Julie's partnership so successful. "What Julie has brought I do not attribute to gender," Tom says. "She has brought tremendous energy and enthusiasm, and an extraordinarily fertile mind that has allowed us to be constantly looking for new ways to do things. I call her my queen of good taste. She has very high standards, and in a way that is more delicate than I would have been, she has helped me create a company where everyone is expected to live up to those standards. I'm talking about behavior, dress and attitude. Julie has brought a collegiality and enthusiasm that's rare in building the organization we have today. One of the great joys and honors of my life is to have the pleasure of working with Julie Smith."

NEIL SHAH AND LILY CUA

Neil Shah and Lily Cua are young entrepreneurs. They are co-founders of Aspire, a smart benefits packaging company that develops sofware which allows HR and employees to customize perks such as fitness, career coaching, day care, and dinner delivery. Their partnership is progressive: Neil is the big-sky idea person and networker, and Lily is the feet on the ground, number-crunching realist. They epitomize the new model of high-performance, gender-neutral culture.

Neil is a serial entrepreneur who was formerly a product developer for Everfi, a leading education technology company focused on teaching, assessing, badging and certifying K–12 and higher education students in critical skills. Previously, he cofounded Compass Partners, an organization that trains social entrepreneurs in college campuses across the world.

Prior to partnering with Neil, Lily Cua was a senior advisory associate in the federal financial management and analysis group at PricewaterhouseCoopers. She specialized in providing strategic workforce planning, performance management and data strategy support to federal agencies.

Neil and Lily met working together at Compass Partners, which gives social entrepreneurs the tools and resources they need to make the world better through the power of entrepreneurship. The Compass Fellowship is a two-year program that connects students with a nationwide community of likeminded peers and gives them the resources to start their own social venture. Compass has been supported by the Prudential Foundation and the Kenneth Cole Foundation, and has also been featured in a variety of news publications from *Fast Company* to *The Washington Post*.

Neil and Lily are talented, hardworking Millennials who are showing us how important it is to change culture to maximize productivity and well-being. They are not the type to sit at a desk all day, but they work harder and more efficiently than most. They are leaders of Generation Y, people aged 18 to 35 who are often in graduate school or beginning their careers. They were interviewed together for this book.

Lily says that she has been fortunate in that she hasn't experienced gender discrimination in the workplace. "I was treated well at PwC," she says. "PwC is progressive that way. They also have flexible work options for men and women such as extensive maternity and paternity leave. It just makes sense to institute policies that benefit talent, regardless of gender."

The idea of benefiting all employees with flexible options is what their new business is all about. Neil says the idea is "that companies need to create more holistic, balanced workplaces for their employees. Our idea is to create a business intelligence tool to help companies to create deeply personalized incentive plans for their employees. We're very excited about it!"

Lily says that their experience and their partnership has not been influenced by typical gender roles. "Transitioning to our partnership has been interesting," she says. "Gender hasn't been a consideration in our partnership—we work well together, and that doesn't have anything to do with the fact that one of us is male and the other is female. We're going into a truly balanced startup. There's a synergy in our approach that works for us. Neil is the big thinker who has an endless flow of ideas, and I focus on how we can execute those ideas to achieve our strategic goals."

"I agree," Neil says. "Our experience doesn't really relate to the discussion about gender difference and imbalanced leadership. Startup cultures are just very different from what we've heard from the previous generations of business. Startups are almost the opposite of big companies with old boys' clubs in leadership. And start-ups are unique in that they don't have much room for fluff. If you help the company with its key metrics, you are a valuable part of the workplace. If you don't, you aren't. Leadership is merit based, not gender based."

> "My generation can talk idealistically about succeeding in our personal and professional lives because we've seen startups thrive, and we have been brought up to always believe that we can achieve the success we define for ourselves, and not let anyone tell us otherwise."
> —Lily Cua

Neil says that the future of the workplace is gender neutral. "Sometimes I feel that conversations around women's issues in the workplace stagnate because people are afraid of being overly politically correct," he says. "It's very clear that it's a good idea to share leadership, but with the best people, regardless of gender. In my view, successful businesses are not just gender balanced, but are gender neutral. Talented people should be in positions of leadership."

Lily agrees, and says that Generation Y might solve many of these gender problems. "Culture change happens generationally," she says. "From my few years of experience working, it seems like Gen Y is almost there, at a culture solution. Maybe we have just been lucky to work with likeminded colleagues, but I am hopeful that we are moving in the right direction towards a gender-neutral workplace. I was brought up by parents who said to me, 'You can do anything.' My generation can talk idealistically about succeeding in our personal and professional lives because we've seen startups thrive, and we have been brought up to always believe that we can achieve the success we define for ourselves, and not let anyone tell us otherwise."

ARTHUR WOODS

Arthur Woods is a social entrepreneur working in operations, design and positive psychology. He believes that in order to address the world's greatest needs, we need to rethink the way that organizations impact and measure the well-being of the people they serve. He cofounded Imperative, a design firm inventing new ways for companies to measure, improve and report social impact. He previously led operations at YouTube EDU, where he focused on initiatives to improve the quality and quantity of educational content on YouTube.

Arthur serves on the board of directors of the Compass Fellowship, the Sierra Institute and Georgetown Technology Alliance. He is also part of the World Economic Forum Global Shapers in New York.

At Imperative, "the focus is on philosophical purpose," Arthur says. "The nature of the U.S. economy has evolved from agricultural to industrial to information. The last forty years the main driver of the economy has been information. People have been marginalized, including women and minorities. Morale is low. It's time to reprioritize and redesign companies with more transparency and purpose. Social enterprises are symbols of the new economy. We're trying to create value for people."

Arthur and his colleagues work with companies like Twitter, LinkedIn and Etsy that understand why change needs to happen and need help implementing that change. Imperative's service model gives tools and resources to operationalize company values, and they show how values translate into the customer experience.

"When we started Imperative," Arthur says, "I was the only guy on the team—it became immediately clear that this would actually set us apart and equip us to do so much more. My colleagues brought to the table a unique perspective and new set of experiences. They uncovered the significance of family, empathy, and brought forth ways in which we could redesign companies to support work-life balance both within an organization and in society generally."

Arthur was recently in a room of corporate leaders who were all older white men, and he was struck by the fact that the majority of the world's most influential companies are still led primarily by older white men. "I realize there are leaders who might be spotting this trend of women in leadership positions, influencing change, but still are unsure what to make of it," he says. "Point blank, the train is leaving the station and you're either on it or you're not."

Look at LinkedIn, Google, Twitter and Etsy. They have a pragmatic vision of talent. These Silicon Valley startups promote women and Millennials who are passionate and performing. These startups are showing tremendous growth because they are designed for this new economy. "It's no longer political," Arthur says. "Times are changing. Women, Millennials and Gen Yers make up a huge market share. You've got to redesign your hierarchy or you will lose your relevancy."

> **"I realize there are leaders who might be spotting this trend of women in leadership positions, influencing change, but still are unsure what to make of it.**
> **Point blank, the train is leaving the station and you're either on it or you're not."**
> **—Arthur Woods**

If you want to be seen as a progressive company, if you want to recruit the best talent, you've got to design for the people you're serving and let your leadership reflect that. Even if you don't believe it yet, the market is demanding shared leadership.

"Legacy models need to be reconsidered," Arthur says. "There is an increasing trend toward virtual work. People ask, is it effective in building community in the workplace? It comes down to trusting your people. Women have a different set of needs. Again, we need to redesign for families. You've got to say, 'We trust you will do well and work hard.' We know that where there's lack of trust, there's low morale. Where there's a lot of trust and flexibility, people perform to the nth degree. Don't assume you can't make it work. With a desire and with good people and today's amazing technology, it can work, and you and your people will be the better for it."

CONCLUSION

Writing this book has been an amazing journey. It has been a privilege and a joy to converse with each person who is part of this book. Each one of them is a remarkable person, highly capable and very caring about others—a true leader! Every one of them exemplifies what leadership is all about. It's attitude.

As we've seen, the best leaders are servant leaders who lead by example, who believe that every team member should be treated with respect and have the opportunity to do meaningful work. We've learned that women and men have equally important skills and strengths that matter greatly. Women leaders help us look at the big picture, collaborate and build sustainable organizational cultures that achieve long-term results. Men lead boldly and decisively. When women and men lead together, our leadership is thoughtful and decisive, with a strong mutual desire to succeed, and the outcome is highly productive culture that drives for results.

Change is coming. Some companies have already diversified and strengthened their leadership and are doing consistently well as a result. Women and men leading together are raising the bar substantially in their companies. This is our opportunity as CEOs and senior managers to be true leaders, to be out in front of this movement, strengthening our leadership with a full array of skills.

Empowerment is critical. If the high-potential women in your company need mentoring and coaching to improve confidence, or stretch opportunities to position themselves for promotion, it is up to you to provide that. Remember, if you have good people and you treat them as teammates and partners, they will feel trusted and happy to be part of your company. They will deliver for you.

We need to provide our people with every advantage, and that means the very best leadership possible! Sharing leadership with accomplished and high-potential women is absolutely the right strategy if we want to remain competitive in the future. Be the leader who helps make this happen within your company. You'll be rewarded with better results, and you'll be respected as a forward-thinking leader! Mentoring, sponsoring, coaching and promoting women will improve internal relations, invigorate our companies and maximize financial results, year after year.

Let's put policies in place right now that will sustain talent and profits.

Let's put policies in place right now that will sustain talent and profits. And let's be sure that these policies are developed thoughtfully and with widespread input, recognizing the different needs of your people and understanding that these needs are dynamic and changing.

Flexible hours, parental leave, working from home and other policy changes are all necessary for women to flourish as professionals and mothers. And it is critically important to recognize that the constant effort that working mothers put forth to keep everything going—to achieve at work and tend to their families at home — can be very demanding and depleting unless they have our support. One way we can support them is to offer opportunities for spiritual fulfillment.

My colleague John Fontana, who directs a program for ethics in business, says that spiritual values are especially important to women.

John says, "I have noticed that women gain greater satisfaction and fulfillment from the workplace when they understand that as leaders, they are orchestrating not just individuals, but also communities. Women will notice the little things and see the enriching dimensions of work. Once they see how the workplace can be transformed from a competitive place to a place of cooperation and camaraderie, women create communities that offer fulfillment and support for all."

Let's remember that working mothers work very hard to get it all done and they are often giving to others all day and well into the night. A time set aside for quiet reflection with a mentor, a pastor or a coach can be deeply meaningful. We need to honor that when we consider women's needs to pursue work and family satisfaction.

Remember, it's essential that everyone in the company realize the importance of attracting and retaining highly capable women, and that women have visible opportunities to use their very important business and leadership skills in key positions of responsibility and authority. Only in this way will women be able to bring their positive influence and energize the spirit of your company. Working with you, side by side, women in the C-suites will improve your company exponentially.

If I were to have a bottom-line recommendation, it is empowerment. Be very clear about expectations and goals and then empower your people. They will work hard to live up to your level of trust.

As Tom Bozzuto said to Julie Smith, "I'm not going tell you how to do this. I know you'll figure it out." Trust your people. Be the leader who inspires them to make your company the very best it can be.

AUTHOR BIO

John Keyser is the founder and CEO of Common Sense Leadership, a leadership consulting and coaching firm. He held senior leadership positions with Johnson & Higgins, Marsh & McLennan, the Damon Runyon Cancer Research Foundation and the Georgetown University Medical Center. He is a graduate of Georgetown University and Georgetown's Institute for Transformational Leadership.

John has a passion for coaching, and is committed to helping businesswomen advance to the C-suites.

John works with senior executives striving to become highly effective leaders - and their best selves. He helps them energize organizational culture by initiating conversations and sharing ideas that inspire teamwork. He has a sincere desire to help executives appreciate the quality of their relationships with their clients and teammates - their internal clients. Empathy, conscious listening, earning trust and kindness are his trademarks.

Now in the Washington, D.C. area, John has previously lived in Chicago and New York. He treasures his relationships with his family and friends.

ACKNOWLEDGMENTS

This book would not be possible without the support and insights of my wife, Leland.

As I wrote this book, I had the benefit of working with Adrienne Hand, a great friend and gifted writer, as my editor. We were a team, and Adrienne is a superb teammate.

There are a great many people who have taught me the enormous value of working alongside very talented women. Through their influence during my career, or their encouragement to this day, they have contributed tremendously to this book.

Carole Sargent, Jeff Chapski, Ron Lippock, Kerry Douglass, Amy Dawson, Cathy Thompson, Andy and Sarah Funt, Sally Seppanen, Cary Larson, Lauree Ostrofsky, Mary Mavis, Emily Clark, Jill Timon, Lulu Gonella, John Fontana, Alisa Parenti, Ann Graham, Celia de la Torre, Amanda Doyle, Ken Tyrrell, Marisa Peacock, Cathy Becker, Al Ritter, Wendy Alexander, Joan Sherman, Regina Hall, Stephanie Berger, Bette June Ingham, Nicole Osborne Ash, Rafe Morrissey, Terri Lakowski, Laura Farina, Diane Tomb, Carolyn Bivens, Susan Alvarado, Rae and David Evans, Sue Mahanor, Bill Curtis, James daSilva, Dana Theus, Amy Gregg Maher, Anne, Harry, Chris and Katie Golski, Cari Sisserson, John Halleron, Lisa Loehr, Leilani Durbin, Zenash Shiferaw, Mike Shevlin, Carolyn Bivens, Larry McGivney, Duncan Ryder, Kathleen DuBois, Jake Styacich, Meagan Barry, Murphy Gallagher, Bob Bies, Julie Creed, Liz Keyser, Angela Hayes, Christine Allen, Cynthia Shafer, Norean Sharpe, Larry Lund, Kate Ebner, Carla D'Andre, Susan Smith Blakley, Julie Cruz, Peter Hill, Julie Foudy Sawyers, Mary Ellen Clark, Julie Shows, Dawn Riley, Tuti Scott, Donna Lopiano, Carol Murphy, David Thomas, Rob Cullen, Courtney Altemus, Chase Reynolds, Becky Wiese, Mary Beall Adler, Rock Tonkel, Russ Reynolds, Robin Kencel, Jim Garland, Bob Lawton, S.J., Bert Getz, Jenn Howard, Allen Lenzner, Molly Williams, Rich Tafel, Dana Alvarez, Massie Valentine, Patti Warble, Roger O'Neill, Gail Ward, John Gussenhoven, Roger Hickey, Dan Altobello, Rita Cheng, Jennifer Young, Katie Coyle, Bill Rehanek, Kathe Ana, Patrick Kilcarr, Sarah Hay, Emily Holland White, Alex Elmore, Dani Davis, Tom Begley, Deb Stalker, Camille Preston, Carol von Stade, Colette Kleitz, Mardi and Pat Hackett, Jerry Egan, Connie Walsh, Jim Rizzo, Linda Platzer, Bryan Bielecki, Valerie Yanni, Jered Wieland, Holly Fake, Bob Beckel, Afy Shahidi, Peggy Hassett, John Walker, Meaghan Feder, Ed Machir, Susy Cheston, Inge Relph, Mary Ellen Russell, Christine Brown-Quinn, Celine Brillet, Anaka Hand, Steve Heller, Matilda Carpenter, Gwyn Meeks, Kristen Kramer, Dan Knise, Katie Brophy, Katie Barongan, Kelly Arensen, Clay Parcells, Ryan Amanda Smith, Michelle Somerday and my classmates from Georgetown and Lawrenceville, the team members of Georgetown's women's golf program while Leland was their coach, my cohort members during the Georgetown Leadership Coaching Program, and friends from when I lived in Bronxville, West Hampton Beach, Winnetka and now Bethesda and Charlevoix, and very definitely my great friends from my years at Johnson & Higgins.

Thank you all. You may not realize how much each of you has helped me.

ENDNOTES

1. A. J. C. Cuddy, M. Kohut and J. Neffinger. "Connect, Then Lead." *Harvard Business Review* (July/August 2013): 55–61. https://hbr.org/2013/07/connect-then-lead.

2. Carmen DeNavas-Walt, Bernadette D. Proctor and Jessica C. Smith. "Income, Poverty, and Health Insurance Coverage in the United States: 2012." U.S. Census Bureau Current Population Report. (Washington, D.C.: U.S. Government Printing Office, 2013): 11.

3. Ernst & Young. "Groundbreakers Study: Diversity an Equation for Success." (Ernst & Young, 2009), http://www.vitalvoices.org/sites/default/files/uploads/Groundbreakers.pdf. For an excellent research summary, see "Board Brief: Why Gender Diversity Matters." www.txwsw.com/pdf/board_brief.pdf.

4. McKinsey & Company. "Gender Diversity: A Corporate Performance Driver." (McKinsey & Company, 2007). 14.

5. McKinsey & Company. "Women at the Top of Corporations: Making It Happen." (McKinsey & Company, 2010), 7. This McKinsey online survey received responses from 772 men and 1,042 women, representing the full range of regions, industries, tenures and functional specialties. McKinsey specialists analyzed financial performance of 362 major companies from European and BRIC countries with two or more women in the corporate board. They found that on the whole such companies are 41% ahead of the sector's average in terms of return on equity and 56% ahead in terms of EBIT (see box "Corporate Financial Performance and Women in Top Management").

6. J. L. Heskett, T. O. Jones, G. W. Loveman, W. E. Sasser and L. A. Schlesinger. "Putting the Service Profit Chain to Work." *Harvard Business Review* (July 2008): 118–29, http://hbr.org/2008/07/putting-the-service-profit-chain-to-work.

7. J. Zenger and J. Folkman. "Are Women Better Leaders Than Men?" *Harvard Business Review* (March 2012). http://blogs.hbr. org/2012/03/a-study-in-leadership-women-do/.

8. Gerzema, John. *The Athena Doctrine: How Women (and the Men Who Think Like Them) Will Rule the Future.* (San Francisco: Jossey-Bass, 2013). Also see Dan Schawbel, "John Gerzema: How Women Will Rule the Future of Work." *Forbes Magazine* April 16, 2013.

9. Cindy Padnos. "High Performance Entrepreneurs: Women in High-Tech." (Oakland, CA: Illuminate Ventures White Paper, 2010).

10. McKinsey & Company. "Gender Diversity in Top Management: Moving Corporate Culture, Moving Boundaries." (McKinsey & Company, 2013).

11. Zenger and Folkman. "Are Women Better Leaders Than Men?"

12. J. Barsh and L. Yee. "Unlocking the Full Potential of Women at Work." McKinsey & Company, 2012)

13. Ernst & Young. "Groundbreakers Study."

14. Colantuono, Susan. *No Ceiling, No Walls: What Women Haven't Been Told About Leadership—from Career Start to the Corporate Boardroom.* (Charlestown, RI: Interlude Productions, 2010). Susan Colantuono's TED talk on this subject has over one million views: www.ted.com/talks/susan_colantuono_the_career_advice_you_probably_didn_t_get?language=en

15. Deloitte. *Unleashing Potential: Women's Initiative Annual Report.* (New York: Deloitte, 2010): 10.

16. Ibid.

17. Gallup. *State of the American Workplace* (2013). http://www.gallup.com/services/178514/state-american-workplace.aspx

18. Gretchen Spreitzer and Christine Porath. "Creating Sustainable Performance." *Harvard Business Review* (January 2012). https://hbr.org/2012/01/creating-sustainable-performance.

19. Laura J. Kray and Michael P. Haselhuhn. "Male Pragmatism in Negotiators' Ethical Reasoning." *Journal of Experimental Social Psychology* 48 (2012): 1124–31.

20. T. Bradberry and L. Su. *Women Feel Smarter.* (San Diego: Talent Smart White Paper, 2008).

21. Tarr-Whelan, Linda. *Women Lead the Way: Your Guide to Stepping Up to Leadership and Changing the World.* (San Francisico: Berrett-Koehler, 2009).

22. Barsh and Yee. "Unlocking the Full Potential of Women in the U.S. Economy." (Washington, D.C.: McKinsey & Company, 2011), http://www.mckinsey.com/client_service/organization/latest_thinking/unlocking_the_full_potential.

23. Svenja O'Donnell and Simon Kennedy. "Women Controlling Consumer Spending Sparse Among Central Bankers." *Bloomberg Business* July 24, 2011.

24. Catalyst. "The Bottom Line: Corporate Performance and Women's Representation on Boards." (Catalyst, 2011).

25. Deloitte. *Unleashing Potential.*

26. Josh Bersin. "Employee Retention Now a Big Issue: Why the Tide Has Turned." LinkedIn, August 16, 2013.

27. The 30 Percent Club Media Release states that the goal of this UK-originated organization is 30% women on FTSE 100 boards by the end of 2015 (http://30percentclub.org/core-beliefs). On April 29, 2014, the 30% Club launched in the U.S. with Peter Grauer, chairman of Bloomberg L.P., serving as U.S. chair.

28. American Express OPEN. *The 2013 State of Women-Owned Businesses Report.* (American Express OPEN, 2013), https://c401345.ssl. cf1.rackcdn.com/wp-content/uploads/2013/03/13ADV-WBI-E-StateOfWomenReport_FINAL.pdf.

29. Deloitte. *The Deloitte Millennial Survey 2014.* (Deloitte, 2014).

30. Babcock, Linda and Laschever, Sara. *Women Don't Ask: The High Price of Avoiding Negotiation.* (New York: Random House, 2007).

31. Jodi Kantor. "Harvard Business School Case Study: Gender Equity." *The New York Times* September 7, 2013. www.nytimes. com/2013/09/08/education/harvard-case-study-gender-equity. html?_r=0.

32. Society for Human Resource Management. *Workplace Flexibility in the 21st Century: Meeting the Needs of the Changing Workforce.* (Society for Human Resource Management Survey Report, 2009). In November 2008, the society for Human Resource Management conducted the SHRM 2008 Workplace Flexibility Survey. The purpose of the survey was to identify: (1) the prevalence and types of flexible work arrangements (FWAs) that employees offer; (2) employee utilization of FWAs; (3) employees that collect metrics/analytics on FWAs; (4) successful FWAs, as well as successful factors; (5) the impact of FWAs on both employees and employers; and (6) the challenges associated with FWAs.

33. Anna Beninger and Nancy Carter. "The Great Debate: Flexibility vs. Face Time - Busting the Myths Behind Flexible Work Arrangements." (Catalyst, 2013), www.catalyst.org/knowledge/great-debate-flexibility-vs-face-time-busting-myths-behind-flexible-work-arrangements. Part of "The Promise of Future Leadership: A Research Program on Highly Talented Employees in the Pipeline." Catalyst Research Series. October, 2012.

34. Sylvia Ann Hewlett, Carolyn Buck Luce, Peggy Shiller, and Sandra Southwell. "Hidden Brain Drain: Off-Ramps and On-Ramps in Wom-

en's Careers." Harvard Business Review Report. February 24, 2005.

35. C. Porath and G. Spreitzer. "Creating Sustainable Performance." *Harvard Business Review* (January/February 2012). https://hbr. org/2012/01/creating-sustainable-performance.

36. Friedman, Stew. *Baby Bust: New Choices for Men and Women in Work and Family.* (Philadelphia: Wharton Digital Press, University of Pennsylvania, 2013).

37. American Management Association. *Coaching: A Global Study of Successful Practices. Current Trends and Future Possibilities 2008–2018.* (New York: American Management Association, 2008). www.opm. gov/WIKI/uploads/docs/Wiki/OPM/training/i4cp-coaching.pdf.

38. Sylvia Ann Hewlett and Carolyn Buck Luce. "Off-Ramps and On-Ramps: Keeping Talented Women on the Road to Success." *Harvard Business Review* (March 2005).

39. Stone, Pamela. *Opting Out? Why Women Really Quit Careers and Head Home.* (Berkeley: University of California Press, 2007). Also see Amy Wittmayer, "Retaining Women in the Workplace." (UNC Executive Development, 2014).

40. Hewlett, Sylvia Ann. *Off-Ramps and On-Ramps: Keeping Talented Women on the Road to Success.* (Boston: Harvard Business School Press, 2007).

41. Pamela Stone. "Gender & Work: Challenging Conventional Wisdom." (Harvard Business School Research Symposium 2013). www. hbs.edu/faculty/conferences/2013-w50-research-symposium/Documents/stone.pdf.

INDEX